As I See It

John H. Lounsbury

NATIONAL MIDDLE SCHOOL ASSOCIATION

nmsa

NATIONAL MIDDLE SCHOOL ASSOCIATION

John H. Lounsbury has been associated with junior high/middle school education since the 1950s. He served as editor of the *Middle School Journal* from 1976 to July 1990 and continues as editor of NMSA's monographs.

This publication is composed of the *Journal* columns which he authored following the 1984 publication of *Middle School Education: As I See It.* In addition, four other contemporary articles are included. Appreciation is expressed to *Educational Horizons*, the Phi Lambda Theta Journal, the National Association of Secondary School Principals, and the Tennessee Association of Middle Schools for permission to include these important articles.

Special thanks is extended to Mary Mitchell for her painstaking work in preparing these selections for printing.

Cover photo by Sam Walton
Printed in the United States of America by
Panaprint, Inc., P. O. Box 10297, Macon, Ga 31297

ISBN: 1-56090-058-X

To Libby—

for fifty years my
one and only

Contents

Foreword

A Compass For A Movement

One of the most delightful items one comes across in life may be a compass. It is fascinating in its consistency, its resolute accuracy, its singularity of purpose. For the length of the middle school movement, from junior high to middle school, John H. Lounsbury has been such a guiding force.

Many of us came to know John through his role as Editor, *Middle School Journal*, and especially through his *Journal* department, "As I See It." Through this feature John spoke to us with quiet eloquence, with moral conviction, with a cajoling tone of the father-figure that he was and is. Woven between the lines of his written word was a singularity of purpose — to improve the education of young adolescents throughout this nation, and eventually, as NMSA expanded to its present shape, to other parts of the world. This singularity of purpose is best captured in what I call "The Lounsbury Postulate." It states:

> If you believe that young adolescents are different
> from young children and older adolescents then the
> schools that serve them should be different as well.

This collection of "As I See It" and other contemporary offerings will provide readers an opportunity to view the work of this leader as a whole entity. For old friends familiar with the *Journal* and John's writing there will be an opportunity to reacquaint oneself with familiar friends, to pick up on a forgotten entry anew. For newer members and readers this monograph provides a historical perspective of a portion of the middle school movement through the eyes of one of its earliest leaders. As well, it touches the question of who we *should be* in the lives of young adolescents. John has pointed the way. This collection is a portion of the road map.

Tom Dickinson, Editor
Middle School Journal

If good men do nothing

The critic's cauldron, first fired by the rhetorical and political report of the Commission on Excellence in Education (1983) has not cooled down. Indeed, many other task force reports have added fuel to the continuing fire. The newspapers continue to give the state of American education ample ink. Public education has even become a campaign issue at the national level. Despite the fact that some reports contain false charges and questionable conclusions, usually presented without benefit of supporting data, the recapturing of the nation's attention by education is, in itself, an extremely positive development. Out of this interest and reflection *could* come a restoration of parental responsibility, a renewed readiness to support financially this great engine of democracy, and a thoughtful examination of school curriculum.

The recapturing of the nation's attention by education is, in itself, an extremely positive development.

But the knee jerk reaction educators feared has taken place. State legislatures and Boards of Education have acted to implement the recommendations presented in *A Nation At Risk* and subsequent reports. Whether these recommendations are appropriate or not for high schools, I will leave to others to debate, but, as I see it, without considerable modification they are most inappropriate for intermediate educational institutions. Yet the over-eager reformer's brush is wide, and, as a result, legitimate and important middle level programs are being excised as the recommendations are applied hastily and indiscriminately. Nowhere in these reports is there any indication that middle level education was even considered. Certainly, then, the often simplistic recommendations, which were in no way differentiated to recognize level, should not be applied below the ninth grade.

Exploratory programs, only recently receiving the attention and school time their importance warrants, seem to be the major early victims. To the casual and uninformed citizen, such programs may seem nice though not necessary, but to anyone who truly understands the

1

nature and needs of young adolescents it is obvious that exploratory programs are basic and of critical importance to the full educational and personal development of youth at this age level.

Middle school educators must not sit back and bemoan the inadequate understandings of early adolescence. Rather they must assume a proactive posture. The heart of the middle school movement is in serious jeopardy as recommendations for the high school are misapplied to the middle level. It behooves those of us who understand middle level education to be fully informed about the various reports and ready to expound on and advance the educational program needed by young adolescents.

Middle school educators must not sit back and bemoan the inadequate understandings of early adolescence. Rather they must assume a proactive posture.

This is not a time to sit on the sidelines. Remember the admonition that Edmund Burke issued in 1795, "The only thing necessary for the triumph of evil is for good men to do nothing."

February, 1984

Put it in writing

Talk is cheap. Oral communication can be and often is confusing. Therefore, education which is carried out primarily through the spoken word has long been characterized by a certain vagueness. The accountability movement is, in many respects, an understandable reaction to the looseness of objectives and procedures which has been characteristic of teaching with its over-reliance on conversation. Since we may have never clarified in any meaningful way exactly what we sought to do or what our philosophical position was, no one could make a clear judgment as to whether or not we had done much, or even if we were heading in the right direction.

Admittedly, we have taken a certain comfort in this situation. The availability of valid reasons why the education of human beings could not be made more objective and subject to exact quality controls gave us an out. The breadth of education's objectives and the magnitude of the task have also been recognized by the public, so we were not often pressed for specificity.

There is, of course, much to be said for teachers and schools having considerable flexibility, for being able to capitalize on the teachable moment, and for holding in abeyance a tight, philosophical position. Professionals ought to have freedom to use their best judgment in plying their craft. Yet, as I see it, we may have taken advantage of this situation, and ought now to become more specific and definite about our beliefs and our purposes.

"How do I know what I think until I see what I say?"
— E. M. Forster

E.M. Forster has commented sagely, "How do I know what I think until I see what I say?" There is a clear and distinct benefit to be derived from putting something in writing. It utilizes the sense of sight as well as that of hearing and it makes ideas available for thoughtful analysis and contemplation, both by oneself and by others. American author, William Faulkner declared: "I have found that the greatest help in meeting any problem with decency and self-respect and whatever courage is demanded is to know where you yourself stand. That is, to have in *words* what you believe and are acting from."

We ought to, individually as teachers and collectively as faculties, commit our basic beliefs to writing.

You become vulnerable when you put something in writing. That is why people resist putting things on paper. To guide educational endeavors properly, however, the clarity and commitment of the written word is of real value. Churches long ago recognized the value of setting forth beliefs in written form. While I am not advocating the adoption of a middle school catechism, I do believe we ought to, individually as teachers and collectively as faculties, commit our basic beliefs to writing.

Putting your philosophy in writing is not just a nice idea or something you have to do as part of a self study. It is a basic and necessary step in the process of achieving a truly effective school. A vibrant, widely accepted, and clear philosophy is a distinguishing characteristic of such schools. Certainly just writing out one's beliefs

---

A vibrant, widely accepted, and clear philosophy is a distinguishing characteristic of effective schools.

---

is not enough, but the chances of implementing a philosophy that has not been put down in black and white are slight. So wrestle with your set of middle school beliefs, firm up your educational philosophy, and put it in writing.

May, 1984

4

The most neglected (and important?) basic

Reading is fundamental. Its importance warrants the special attention it receives. As a basic, it is a given and I'm not advocating a reduction in the emphasis it receives. But, as I see it, oral communication may be the most neglected skill, and, in many respects, it may be the most important.

Outside of school, students do not wear a label revealing their reading levels for all the world to see, but when a student or former student opens his mouth to communicate orally, a "score" is being computed, however unconsciously, by all who hear. Jobs are regularly won, or lost, on the basis of effectiveness in oral communication, rarely, if ever, on the basis of reading level. The admonition Shakespeare offered in *Othello*, "mend your speech a little, lest it mar your fortunes," might well be recalled and heeded.

The opportunities and capabilities for communicating with others have never been greater. Almost anyone is likely to be on camera and engaged in an impromptu interview, on the street, at the scene of an accident, or at a sporting event. Thus the inadequacies of most Americans, including many public figures, in expressing themselves are readily and painfully apparent. Whether television is a major cause or not, it does seem clear that Americans have lost much of their interest in and their effectiveness in oral communication.

We talk about what we talk about, but we seldom talk about talk.

In school, speaking and listening comprise up to 90 percent of the time. In the out-of-school world as much as 75 percent of the time may be spent in talking or listening to someone else talk. Yet how much time does the school give to teaching listening and effective oral communication? We talk about what we talk about, but we seldom talk about talk.

It is somewhat difficult to explain the neglect of oral communication. Somehow people think that oral language and listening come naturally, are already in place, and are unalterable. We painstakingly check students' numerical calculations, we edit and make them improve their written work, but beyond an urging to speak louder, we offer little constructive criticism or instruction to help them become more articulate.

Efforts to improve students' oral communication are not primarily designed to increase their marketability or social competence, although they will do both of these things. Instruction in oral communication contributes directly to the central objective of American education — critical thinking. Language is the raw material we use in thinking, and sloppy language leads to sloppy thinking.

Instruction in oral communication contributes directly to the central objective of American education — critical thinking.

A further justification for giving increased attention to speaking in middle school classrooms was reported by Sears and Navin (*Middle School Journal*, November, 1982, pp. 19-20). The number one stress factor reported by these researchers was speaking in front of the class. The natural and increased self-consciousness of young adolescents is heightened even more by an inadequacy that is based on lack of instruction and adequate opportunity to speak in low-risk situations. Given proper conditions, the self-concepts of middle level youngsters can be boosted rather than booted by "oral reports."

So consider giving some specific time and attention to the improvement of oral communication. I believe the results of such efforts, particularly if mounted on a faculty-wide basis, will be quickly evident and will lead to a gain in reading itself.

August, 1984

The overlooked key to school improvement

Schools need to be improved. Few would argue otherwise. This is not to say that schools are not as good as they used to be. That issue is of no consequence and is really not resolvable, but I have to respond negatively to the question, "Are schools as good as they need to be to prepare youth for effective and satisfying lives today?"

The responsibilities given to public education in a time when the culture provides so many counter lessons and so little moral and financial support are awesome. That all is not well in public education, then, is not surprising. So the many recommendations made by national commissions and task forces are given considerable publicity and are readily endorsed. Boards of Education take satisfaction in actions increasing graduation requirements, adding more "academic" courses, purchasing more computers, even hiring more teachers.

Student achievement, like morality, is not easily legislated.

All such actions may be desirable under certain circumstances, but unless accompanied by a more supportive climate and an improved social context, they may effect little significant improvement, certainly not at the middle level. They give the appearance of improvement and provide some comfort for concerned parents, but they do not come to grips with the heart of the problem. Student achievement, like morality, is not easily legislated.

As I review the various reports released during 1983 and 1984, I am struck by the realization that the recommendations made seem to overlook what is, as I see it, ultimately the real key to improving education — the students themselves !

In Georgia, former Governor Lester Maddox was widely ridiculed and belittled for his remark that the way to improve the troubled prisons in Georgia was to have a better class of prisoners. But you know,

7

there may be a legitimate point in there somewhere, for I believe that the best way to improve schools is to improve the students themselves.

The best way to improve schools is to improve the students themselves.

If we would institute changes in teaching procedures that would alter the attitudes of students, that would tap their internal and inherent motivators, that would involve them more genuinely in the teaching-learning process, that would utilize them as agents of instruction, that would challenge them, pique their natural curiosity, and make more evident our concern and respect for them as persons of worth — if we would do these sorts of things we would alter the attitudes and behavior of students in positive ways. Unnecessary, then, would be "tougher" requirements or simplistic increases in the volume of homework.

"The real curriculum is the one the pupil experiences."   *— Kimball Wiles*

Students, after all, learn what they want to learn. As the late Kimball Wiles pointed out: "The real curriculum is the one the pupil experiences. Actually the expectations of curriculum designers may be illusions and the teachers' guides and syllabi mere paper representations of hollow hopes." To really improve the education which our youth are receiving we should look to intrinsic means rather than depending so much on extrinsic ones. Working directly on the self-concepts and attitudes of students will yield greater returns, academically and otherwise, than imposed demands.

November, 1984

8

CAUTION—danger ahead

The pressure to cover content is mounting. Teachers feel it. Scores on achievements tests are under increased scrutiny. Administrators can attest to this. New state regulations and curriculum prescriptions are being issued. Curriculum directors have the memoranda from Capital City in hand as evidence. While I understand the climate which gives rise to these conditions, and I too share a concern for educational excellence, I am apprehensive about the possible effects of current pressures on middle schools.

Curriculum prescriptions, no matter how well-intentioned, may well hinder middle level teachers in meeting the intellectual needs of their pupils. While redesigned courses of study may be conscientiously constructed and even be appropriate for pupils "in general," they can be counter productive when taught to young adolescents whose principal characteristic is their diversity.

> *Curriculum prescriptions, no matter how well-intentioned, may well hinder middle level teachers in meeting the intellectual needs of their pupils.*

Professional teachers who are in direct and daily contact with specific students, who know their backgrounds and track records, and who are sensitive to their interests and emotions, ought not be hampered unduly in exercising their professional judgment about what, when, and how to teach.

I do not advocate unlimited license or a laissez-faire approach to content. Our marvelous mass education system does need textbooks, curriculum guides, common requirements, and a basic framework of scope and sequence. But I am fearful that, given the current climate, teachers will feel compelled to relinquish much of their professional judgment and creativity and knuckle-under narrowly conceived and highly specific content objectives which are purported to yield improved test scores. Unfortunately, an orderly presentation of a canned curriculum does not necessarily correlate well with excellence at the middle level.

The best middle school teachers are more nearly artists than technicians, and they need to adjust their teaching constantly in recognition of the varying interests and abilities of their in-transition pupils.

The best middle school teachers are more nearly artists than technicians.

There is as well the danger that the very heart will be taken out of learning as too zealous efforts are instituted to insure complete coverage. An overly-organized presentation can be detrimental to real learning. It is true that learning proceeds best when learners feel reasonably confident that they can accomplish what is expected of them. However, making things too clear, too routinized, can keep learning at the level of rote memorization and surface acceptance.

There is a delicate balance between making things too clear on the one hand and making things too vague and difficult on the other. What is needed is neither easy learning nor impossible learning, but challenging learning. A chief motivating element is the teasing value of uncertainty, the presentation of issues that are conjectural rather than the laying out in recipe format of hard, dry finished facts. There is an inward lure to discovery learning. Someone has stated the principle that "the optional level of difficulty is that one which allows the student to win success *after* difficulty." Middle level pupils, many of whom are beginning to evidence new intellectual prowess, should not be denied challenging learning in an effort to "master" prescribed content.

"The optional level of difficulty is that one which allows the student to win success after difficulty."

Do not, then, be pressured into upping the pace of content coverage or inappropriately accepting a new curriculum package. The ultimate goal of education remains the development of critical thinking.

February, 1985

10

It's up to us

"There is nothing more difficult to take in hand, more perilous to conduct, or more uncertain in its success, than to take the lead in the introduction of a new order of things."

These words of Machiavelli should give us a perspective by which to assess the status of the middle school movement. Nobody said that implementing the middle school concept — truly a new order of things — would be easy. And it hasn't been. But, on balance, significant progress has been made and prospects for the future are bright.

I am challenged by the occasional, somewhat pessimistic views of the middle school movement sometimes heard. Some express concern over the lack of progress and wonder if the movement would die.

I've often been accused, and rightly so, of being an optimist, yet I cannot write off because of my naivety the belief that the middle school concept is gaining acceptance and is influencing positively the quality of education early adolescents are experiencing. I'm well aware of the paucity of middle level teacher education programs, of the entrenched status of departmentalization, of the obsession over achievement of subject matter *per se* held by many, of the pressure teachers face to have students score well on standardized tests, and all the rest. I do battle with these realities regularly. But I am also aware of the growing body of research that does support the middle school concept, of the spirit I sense among middle level teachers and principals who are professionals and who do understand the nature of young adolescents. Even when Boards of Education move to reorganize solely for economic or enrollment reasons, I see serious efforts being made to utilize these opportunities for instituting improved educational practices. More and more middle level schools are moving toward implementing accepted practices.

What lies ahead is up to us. While success is never assured, neither are we ever doomed to failure.

Max Lerner, distinguished author and professor, refuses to call himself either an optimist or a pessimist. He prefers to label himself a "possibilist." This is his way of saying that what lies ahead is up to us. While success is never assured, neither are we ever doomed to failure. Our fate is not in the stars, but in our hands. The future can be and will be determined by those of us with both convictions and the courage to advance those convictions in the market place.

I am moved to keep the faith, ultimately, by one basic belief — that what the middle school concept advocates is rooted in the realities of human growth and development. To my knowledge, every specific practice advanced grows out of our best understanding of the nature of the age group and the principles of learning. On the other hand, the failures of middle level schools to be what they ought to be lie in tradition, administrative factors, the human inclination to resist change, and the lack of understanding of young adolescents, not in the validity of the advocacy.

What the middle school concept advocates is rooted in the realities of human growth and development. On the other hand, failures to implement it lie in tradition, administrative factors, resistance to change, and the lack of understanding of young adolescents, not in the validity of the concept.

So don't be disheartened. We are on the right track. Stay on it. The middle school is not just an educational fad. It is the composite of valid beliefs which are making their way gradually, but perceptively, against the forces of ignorance and tradition, as well as apathy. Let us all, then, dare to do our duty, to commit ourselves to actively supporting what we know young adolescents need; for, as Abraham Lincoln pointed out, right does make might.

May, 1985

New school year's resolutions

If this is August can school be far behind? Pre-planning will soon be upon us and we'll be caught up in counting textbooks, arranging bulletin boards, reviewing new administrative policies, and otherwise getting ready to begin a new year of middle level teaching. There is a lot to do, but there is time, and we must take it, to think seriously and professionally about the upcoming year. We might ask, "How can I as an individual teacher make this year even better than last year for my pupils — and for myself?" or "How can we as a faculty improve the overall effectiveness of our school?"

While I recognize fully the ephemeral nature of resolutions, I would nevertheless challenge each professional staff member to make one personal resolution for the school year, and likewise challenge each school faculty to agree on one area on which it will focus its curriculum improvement efforts in the coming year.

This is not too much to expect of professional people engaged in the most important business there is, education, for a group, young adolescents, going through the most critical time of life. And the time is right, for middle level education has survived infancy and early childhood and is growing rapidly into independence. It has established itself as distinctive and is gaining long overdue recognition. We are caught up in the most exciting and engaging major educational movement now in existence — one that is truly making a difference. It would be a shame to be a part of this educational movement and not take an active part in it.

It would be a shame to be a part of this educational movement and not take an active part in it.

Each teacher, each faculty, will have to decide on what resolutions to adopt. To stimulate thinking let me propose some possibilities.

For individual teachers

1. I resolve to take time to really teach critical thinking. Since this is the central objective of American education, I will urge my pupils to think, to analyze, to go beyond the simple correct answer, to examine alternatives — even at the expense of "covering" content.

2. I resolve to take time to clarify purposes, both for long range plans and daily activities. Recognizing that many early adolescents do not perceive any need to learn what we want to teach them, that their priorities are necessarily elsewhere, I will assist them in recognizing the specific objectives and purposes for the materials being studied and in understanding the procedures being utilized.

For school faculties

1. We resolve to make a greater effort to communicate with parents, to share information with them without asking anything of them, to contact them with positive reports before we have to contact them with problems. Each faculty member will make at least one positive parent contact each week.

2. We resolve to make common and concerted efforts to help pupils improve their use of the communication skills, not by isolated efforts to correct deficiencies, but by the functional use of these skills in all subjects and classes, combined with appropriate instruction.

Other possible resolutions, pertinent to a particular situation, should be easily identified. In order to adequately focus our personal and professional improvement thrusts, then, I urge all of us to hang up clearly defined targets so that we can aim our efforts and thus record discernable progress by the year's end.

August, 1985

Do your own work?

The direction, "Do your own work," is frequently heard in classrooms at every grade level. Even when little preschool children play school, the "teacher" can be heard giving this command along with "Stay in your seat" and "Be quiet." It's part of the culture's stereotype, deeply imbedded in the tradition of formal education. When given at the time of a test it is appropriate, but it is too often used and is tied to procedures which actually restrict learning. At the middle level, especially, we should be encouraging students to work together and learn together.

At the middle level, especially, we should be encouraging students to work together and learn together.

Young adolescents are very much social beings. When in school their great desire is to socialize, to communicate with one another. The most satisfying reward teachers can give students in school is time to talk to their friends. Lunch period is the highlight of the school day, not so much because of the food which feeds physical hunger but because of the interpersonal interaction which feeds social hunger. (And surely the ultimate in animated socialization is a group of seventh or eighth grade girls around a table at lunch.)

Middle level students are in the throes of establishing themselves as social beings, building individual identities on the one hand while becoming accepted parts of the crowd on the other hand. They will engage in socialization, with or without permission. Whispering is practically an art form among early adolescents and they will even resort to writing — often a reluctantly accepted school task — when the need to communicate is present and cannot otherwise be met.

The socialization drive can be academically productive when properly channeled.

It seems strange, then, that at this time of heightened interest in socialization, we in education keep insisting that every one do his or her own work. The socialization drive can be academically productive when properly channeled. Teams of three, four, or more can study together, help one another, even take a test together, and ultimately learn more than if they were made to read and study by themselves.

Not only is more content mastered, but a number of other middle level educational objectives are served by cooperative learning. Opportunities to learn together aid in establishing meaningful social

---

A number of middle level educational objectives are served by cooperative learning.

---

relationships with various age mates of both sexes. They provide chances to consider value related matters and acquire appreciation for the contributions of others while gaining higher self-esteem. They help young adolescents understand how groups operate and provide opportunities for experimenting with leadership skills. They even aid in developing more positive attitudes toward school itself.

Middle level teachers would do well, then, to plan many learning activities that are built around team learning. Pairs, triads, quartets, quintets, rows, all can be utilized at one time or another as a basis for attacking the subject matter at hand. So next time you give an in-class assignment and start to say, "Do your own work," consider letting them work together.

November, 1985

An open letter to administrators and board members

While teachers' salaries are far lower than they ought to be and instructional resources are often in short supply, the most critical condition surrounding teaching today involves neither money nor materials, but recognition and professional status. We ask so much of our teachers but give them so little moral support and treat them in ways which ignore, if not demean, their professional preparation and competence.

> *We ask so much of our teachers but give them so little moral support and treat them in ways which ignore, if not demean, their professional preparation and competence.*

The need to improve public education has worked its way up on America's agenda to a place of such prominence that actions, however inappropriate some of them may be, have had to be taken. While some changes are needed at all levels of schooling, there is an urgency about the middle level for, as those of us involved in middle level education know full well, there is a critical, life-long importance to the kind of educational experiences youth have at this stage of life.

The reform movement has already led to specific actions in nearly every state and school district in the land. But it is not possible to legislate or mandate school improvement. Legislative actions and board of education policies are, at best, only preliminaries to the real educational event, the interaction of students and a teacher in a classroom. Such actions and policies are often very necessary steps, essential beginning points for reform, but they are never, in themselves, the precursors of change that they are commonly thought to be.

In the classroom, only two factors or conditions are really critical: the readiness or motivation of students and the effectiveness of the individual teacher. That sense of personal responsibility to learn, that positive attitude hoped for in students, is primarily in the hands of parents and is only partially affected by the school. The teacher's effectiveness, on the other hand, is more nearly under the influence of the school.

The most direct way to improve education, then, is to improve the personal effectiveness of individual teachers. But how can this be accomplished? Higher entrance requirements for pre-service teachers, tests to screen the knowledge possessed by teachers, required attendance at inservice programs, the installation of teacher-proof curriculum packages, these are some of the ways currently being put forth as means of improving education.

The most direct way to improve education is to improve the personal effectiveness of individual teachers.

There is some merit in each suggestion, but no one of them is able to affect the changes needed, and even in concert they would not spell success. They do not deal sufficiently with the heart of the matter. Even after those few truly incompetent teachers have been weeded out, as they surely should be, the situation will not be drastically different.

The best means of improving education is all too seldom employed. To increase the effectiveness of teachers, as I see it, we need to release their professional potential, tap the commitment that has kept them on the job under less than supportive conditions, utilize more adequately the professional preparation they have undergone, and invest in them the decision-making responsibility that is properly theirs.

To increase the effectiveness of teachers we need to release their professional potential and invest in them the decision-making responsibility that is properly theirs.

If you as administrators and board members are serious about improving education, I urge the implementation of such actions as the following:

1. Professional leave policies with financial support should be instigated so that classroom teachers can participate in appropriate professional conferences. It is a sad commentary when teachers cannot even get a hearing when requesting professional leave for professional development. Yet it often occurs. (A reason that teachers sometimes misuse their personal and sick leave is the subservient manner in which they are treated — which is not at all unlike the way students behave.)

2. Teachers should be given an increased and meaningful role in developing school policy and determining curriculum. This will counter the often well-entrenched atmosphere of "boss and workers" and enhance the correct but dormant climate of collegiality. Effective school research has emphasized anew the importance of teachers having a sense of ownership.

3. Provide relief from some of the time-consuming, relatively petty, and non-professional duties of teachers. Whether by paid aides, volunteer parents, or imaginative administrative leadership a reduction in the non-instructional responsibilities of teachers needs to occur.

4. Provide small grants to a teacher or group of teachers who want to experiment with a new program, technique or special activity. You will thus encourage initiative, vision, and the professional growth which will lead to improvement in student learning.

5. Do not act on any regulation or program revision without first assessing carefully the implications of the proposal at the classroom level and involving teachers in its *initial* analysis.

If middle schools are to be successful that success can and will come only in one place — the classroom.

If middle schools are to be successful that success can and will come only in one place — the classroom. So, administrators and board members, invest your efforts and your resources in the person of the teacher. New requirements and regulations may look good to the general public, but they are a long way removed from the classroom.

Good middle schools are especially dependent on professional teachers, ones who are able and willing to make sound curriculum and procedure decisions as they interact with their varied and ever-changing charges. Do all you can to add to the professional stature of teachers, to empower them, to build up their self-concepts so they, in turn, can guide effectively the development of the young men and women with whom they are privileged to work.

February, 1986

Attitude adjustment

An increasingly negative attitude toward school and school work is widely recognized as a condition that develops for a significant portion of the students between the fifth and eighth grades. The fact that students generally become less "taken" with school work during this period has long been known, and has frequently been documented by research studies. Unfortunately, neither the causes nor the identification of corrective measures have been ascertained in any satisfactory way. A fatalistic assumption that such a condition is inevitable usually takes hold.

A study conducted in Sweden by Lizbeth Hedelin and Lennart Sjoberg reveals what may be the basic cause of this reduced enthusiasm for school. The researchers discovered that not only did students' interest in and attitude toward school lessen markedly as they move through these years, but *students perceived they had much less interaction with teachers than they previously experienced.* Students' perceptions of personal interactions with teachers apparently play a major role in determining their attitudes toward school. Students' self-esteem and feelings of well-being are correlated closely with the level of interaction with teachers and greatly affect both attitude and interest. Attitude and interest, we know, ultimately, relate to achievement — as much or more than intellectual capacity *per se.*

The instructional program should be so organized and conducted that teachers and students can interact more personally.

To avoid the usual deterioration of attitude toward school, then, the instructional program should be so organized and conducted that teachers and students can interact more personally. Keeping teachers and students together for more than one period a day or over a period of more than one year will help to do this. So too will efforts of teachers to initiate individual conversations with pupils, both in and out of the classroom, and to reduce seat work.

21

The installation of departmentalization coincides exactly with this loss of enthusiasm for school. This inevitably gives rise to the question of causality. Installed to insure the mastery of content in the junior high school grades, departmentalization has become a handicap to that achievement as well as to the furtherance of interactions between the teacher and student.

The installation of departmentalization coincides exactly with this loss of enthusiasm for school.

The whole young adolescent, like the whole child, goes to school, and though administratively we may compartmentalize the day to provide direct instruction in the several subjects without recognizing the social-emotional factors at work, we do so at a high price. Academic excellence, as I see it, is more nearly the result of attitude than it is of separate, specialized instruction in the basic subjects. While what students know is very important, we must recognize that their *behavior* is controlled by feelings and attitudes.

We would achieve more effectively the generally recognized academic goals of middle school education themselves if we would slow down in our push to cover content and interact more with students, concerning ourselves with their attitudes as well as their achievement. The middle school's advocacy of interdisciplinary teaming, the affective as a curriculum component, and exploratory programs are all important means to maintain continuing personal interaction with pupils.

We would achieve the academic goals of middle school education more effectively if we would slow down in our push to cover content, interact more with students, and concern ourselves with attitudes as well as achievement.

It is in the advisee-adviser program, of course, that the middle school most directly deals with the psycho-social development of students. It is in this effort that relatively intimate student-teacher interactions are assured. It is here that the development of a "significant other" relationship is nurtured. It is here that an open forum is assured, wherein the real and legitimate concerns of youth can be discussed among peers under the guidance of a mature adult. It is here that students are given opportunities to develop social skills and to experiment with roles and relationships as they develop their own personalities.

The major components or characteristics of the middle school model all enhance positive student-teacher relationships. Perhaps when this model is widely and fully implemented, the traditional loss of enthusiasm toward school that occurs during the middle school years will become a thing of the past.

May, 1986

The challenge
of new realities

When Ron Mitchell was president of the Minnesota Association of Middle Level Educators, he was asked, "What is the biggest concern in your school today?" His answer, as reported in the May 1986 *Newsletter* of the MAMLE, was, "the changing family life of our students and the effect it has on them."

This, it seems to me, is, at once, a significant, a frightening, a valid, and a challenging statement. Perhaps we as educators ought to spend considerable time and effort seriously assessing the new realities of demography, family life, and economics as they relate to a particular student body. Such a study should help to determine what changes in a middle school's role, its procedures and its curriculum are called for, as surely some will be.

Given the already overwhelming burdens which the school in the middle carries, one hesitates to suggest another set of responsibilities, but a thoughtful look at the out-of-school life of our young adolescents may make mandatory, however regrettable, some shifts in priorities and programs.

A thoughtful look at the out-of-school life of our young adolescents may make mandatory, some shifts in priorities and programs.

Harold Hodgkinson of the Institute for Educational Leadership in the 1985 publication, *All One System: Demographics of Education - Kindergarten Through Graduate School,* reports these striking conditions and trends regarding family status:

In 1955, 60% of the households in the U.S. consisted of a working father, a housewife mother, and two or more school age children. In 1980, that family unit made up only 11%, and in 1985, it was only 7%!

More than 50% of the women are in the work force (almost 70% if you consider working-age women).

Fifty-nine (59) percent of the children born in 1983 will live with only one parent before reaching age 18 — this now becomes the normal childhood experience.

The increase in the number of children born outside of marriage is of epidemic proportions — and 50% of such children are born to teenage mothers.

Other reports in news magazines and on television have pointed out the continuing high rate of divorce and its often devastating effects on children, the latchkey millions who spend the late afternoons alone or without appropriate supervision, and the rapid rise in incidences of family violence, child abuse, and substance abuse. More children are growing up in relative poverty, under the care of adolescent mothers. Such children are likely to be shortchanged in both physical and psychological nutrition.

Faculties are faced with a growing number of students who have special needs that impinge on their ability to learn.

Faculties are thus faced with a growing number of students who have special needs, needs that call for special understanding, for extra effort and time, needs that impinge on their ability to learn even if they are not directly related to ability as such. The home life of many seems to be a root cause, though certainly not the sole cause. A seeming lack of personal responsibility and a nonchalance characterize youth today, regardless of whether they are affluent or indigent, majority or minority.

The school's number one mission is, and must remain, the development of the intellect, but in order to be successful in that primary mission it seems certain that the school will have to concern itself even more than it is currently doing with those social and psychological factors that largely control the ability or readiness to achieve academically. Student attitudes, student self-concepts, opportunities for young people to dialogue about current social issues, and the ability and willingness of parents to support the school's agenda, are among things that need to be given more direct attention in the middle school. So too are a greater concern for process, for full discussion of real issues, for developing responsibility, and for acquiring those coping skills that carry over into high school and life. These kinds of things may need to be given greater attention, even at the expense of covering some textbook content.

The school will have to concern itself even more than it is currently doing with those social and psychological factors that largely control the ability or readiness to achieve academically.

The facts are in, distressing as they may be. Family life has changed. Growing up is more complex and difficult. As professional middle level educators we cannot simply wring our hands. We have to give serious attention to these new realities and make needed adjustments in our program and procedures. This school year could well be devoted to wrestling with the changing American family and how we should serve its children.

August, 1986

Moving the school in the middle from the bottom to the top

About the impact of middle level institutions on school organization there can be no doubt whatsoever. The numerical growth of middle level schools is an all-American success story. By the 1940s, the 6-3-3 had become the most common single school organizational pattern in America. And if it were not for those districts where limited enrollment makes a separate middle level school impractical separate intermediate units, now most frequently made up of grades 6-8, would be close to universal realities.

Insufficient understanding of the unique mission of the middle level institution — both by the public and the profession — has and still does plague it.

The presence, indeed the dominance of middle level institutions, regardless of whether they carry the label of *junior high school* or *middle school*, is affirmed in nearly every state. Regrettably, this wide and extensive existence has not been accompanied by an adequate identity. Insufficient understanding of the unique mission of the middle level institution — both by the public and the profession — has and still does plague it. Despite the undeniable success of the reorganization movement, in too many ways, within and without the profession, the middle level is still treated as a step-child. Only a few state departments have established distinctive certification for those who teach at this level. Even fewer have a professional staff member with specific and exclusive responsibilities for the middle level. The strong hand of high school traditions and practices still presses on and too often molds the middle level school.

This situation would not be so serious were it not for the highly critical role of middle level education. No other grades are of more

27

enduring importance. The educational and human impact of these grades exceeds that of the senior high school. These are the prime time years, the years during which one's value system, one's behavior code, and one's self-esteem are largely formed. When the adolescent leaves the middle level institution his or her personality and personal values are largely set — for life. For this reason alone, middle level education desperately needs and clearly deserves greater appreciation and understanding.

The educational and human impact of the middle level grades exceeds that of the senior high school.

To help achieve the needed recognition the National Association of Secondary School Principals, through its Middle Level Council, initiated *National Middle Level Education Week* in 1987 and has continued it annually since then with NMSA as a co-sponsor. A variety of activities have been used to call attention to the special role of schools in the middle. Proclamations, news releases, and other activities have been employed to help promote the movement.

This week provides an opportunity for every junior high school, middle school, intermediate school, and any school incorporating grades 6, 7, or 8 to become proactive in the effort to earn for the middle level long overdue recognition. No school district, no intermediate school, no state should let the occasion pass without expending special effort to join the national celebration.

Middle level schools can make their presence felt by activities such as open houses, coffees for parents, special issues of system or school newsletters, articles for the local paper, mayor's proclamations, presentations to civic groups, student productions, and radio and TV spots. A task force should be established to direct the efforts of a school, district, and/or community in the celebration of National Middle Level Education Week. It is an opportunity middle level educators should not let slip by. The enduring importance of educational experiences during early adolescence call for the best efforts of all concerned. It's time to move the school in the middle from the bottom where it's been, to the top where it belongs.

February, 1987

28

Wayside teaching

Formal, organized instruction is and ought to be the major component of the educational process. It deserves our best attention and our most thoughtful planning. The important place that planned instruction has in the school day is highly evident; bells signal the beginning and the endings of time allotments established for its occurrence and the school day is almost completely given over to it.

While not seeking to deprecate this formal teaching or diminish its primary place in the educational enterprise, I believe there is much more to middle level education than organized instruction. The more influential aspect of middle school education is often what might be called *wayside teaching.* By wayside teaching I mean the teaching that is done between classes, when walking in the halls, after school, and in dozens and dozens of one-on-one encounters, however brief. For principals it is usually the main means of teaching.

There is much more to middle level education than organized instruction.

When all is said and done, what is said informally and casually may have more impact on a person's behavior than what is said formally while instructing a class or conducting a faculty meeting. A response to a student's non-academic question, given spontaneously and without particular forethought, can have great impact. In terms of effecting behavior, such a response may be the most influential act a teacher performs all day. Wayside utterances are often heard at a deeper level than classroom pronouncements.

Fortunately, middle level teachers do not think of themselves as "on duty" only when standing in front of a class. The casual walk with a student or two on the way to a student council meeting is recognized as an opportunity to develop the kind of personal relationship that underlies true excellence in middle level education. The unplanned after-school encounter with a discouraged student is seized as an occasion to express caring and offer a reassuring word. Even a surprise meeting in the mall on a Saturday is seen as a chance to communicate a genuine interest in a student as a worthy person.

Wayside teaching, however, is neither as casual nor as completely accidental as it may appear. Preparation of the heart as well as the mind has to precede it. If teachers have credence with pupils, they will often seek opportunities to engage students in conversation, and vice versa.

While the occasion may come up suddenly and unexpectedly, the quality of the relationship preceding the conversation will reflect a bent of the heart and spirit that usually was a long time in the making.

As middle level educators we cannot evade the responsibility that is inherent in our personal example — and we shouldn't try to.

As middle level educators we cannot evade the responsibility that is inherent in our personal example — and we shouldn't try to. We may not dwell on it a great deal — that would seem self-righteous, even egotistical — but we need to be sensitive to the effect our behavior has on students and faculty.

Our conscious influence, when we are on dress parade, instructing a group, playing the role of teacher, may be relatively small compared to the impact of our wayside teaching. The silent, subtle radiation of one's personality, the effects on one's spontaneous words and unplanned deeds apart from those times when one is in front of the class have great impact. One rarely becomes a "significant other" on the basis of actions when formally instructing. It is in the relationships developed in wayside teaching that one is most likely to influence the lives of others.

May, 1987

30

Can we "fix" the schools?

Thousands of educators, legislators, parents, and others believe our educational problems can be solved by "fixing" the schools. I operate on that assumption myself much of the time. Practically all of us in education act as if we could make the needed difference by altering the curriculum, adding an innovative program, encouraging the use of more effective methods, developing more responsive leadership, and/or enhancing human relationships. Some success is experienced through these means, however little and fleeting it may be, so I intend to continue my efforts to utilize such approaches, and I hope others will as well.

We cannot really solve our educational problems without improving the quality of life outside of school.

However, in my more reflective and sober moments, I often come up against a truth, a hard truth, one that I believe we not only need to face up to but one we should openly deal with. As I see it, we cannot really solve our educational problems without improving the quality of life outside of school. School reform efforts which do not recognize this reality will do little to make a lasting difference, I fear.

The evidence to support this proposition is abundant. Consider the educational innovations and special programs developed and implemented in the last thirty years — the dollars invested in them and the man and woman hours given over to them — yet the educational level of our population has not risen. Student attitudes and behavior have deteriorated.

The really tough problems which we face in education are not caused by inept teachers, inadequate materials, or inappropriate curriculum. Schools are the victims more than the cause of the malaise which surrounds education today. Schools are certainly not without blame, but they are by no means the villains many assume.

31

Schools are the victims more than the cause of the malaise which surrounds education.

The root causes of most of the difficulties teachers face grow out of the quality of life which our young people experience when not in school. The solutions, then, also lie largely outside of the school. Demographic data make apparent the dramatic changes that have taken place in our society. These changes, without exception, impact education and alter the nature of our student body, our objectives, and the mission of the school.

Building better school/community relationships has become a responsibility of the utmost importance. Only as we build back the strong bond that once existed between these two agencies can we bring about the improvements needed in American education. Parent involvement and school/business cooperation are not extra duties to be performed if time permits, they are fundamental and basic ways to improve education. We need to broaden our view of educational problems and direct some of our efforts, both directly and indirectly, at the community, to the world beyond the classroom.

We need to broaden our view of educational problems and direct efforts to the world beyond the classroom.

Directly, we can do more to help parents understand their children and how they must be and can be partners in the educational process. Indirectly, we can teach so that changed behavior is our acknowledged goal, so that our graduates will become a part of the solution rather than the problem. We can select subject matter that is truly relevant and relate our lessons to contemporary life and community issues.

Every middle school faculty might well devote time to consider what, through the collective efforts of faculty and staff, could be done to impact positively the out-of-school lives of their students.

August, 1987

Pogo revisited

"We have met the enemy and he is us."

Few bits of conventional wisdom have been as frequently quoted, or have become more ingrained in our contemporary culture's folklore than this catchy, however ungrammatical, maxim that first appeared in the comic strip, *Pogo*. It contains an unvarnished truth, but states it in such a clever way that few take offense, even when they know that it applies to them.

In education, as in most other aspects of life, we are our own worst enemies. Masters of deceit and rationalizing, we humans conjure up all sorts of excuses that supposedly shift the blame to others — the school administration, the State Department of Education, parents, society in general.

Because the easiest person to deceive is one's self, we take advantage of that proclivity, but usually know all along, in our heart of hearts, that we aren't even fooling ourselves. We still hope, however, that we are fooling others and that they will accept our explanations. But Pogo was on target when he pointed the finger at us and claimed we were to blame. Our attitudes and actions, individually and collectively, are usually the source of problems as much as the pre-existing conditions.

This column, however, is not designed to reinforce the central point of Pogo's adage, to amplify his put-down; rather it is to call attention to the other side of Pogo's proverb. While we may be the cause of most of our problems we are, at the same time, the real source of the solutions in almost all cases.

While we may be the cause of most of our problems we are, at the same time, the real source of the solutions in almost all cases.

Though we look for easy answers, organizational solutions, corrective measures that can be purchased, and teacher-proof

33

curriculums, we know that effective schools are the result of effective teaching, not just effective organizations, effective materials, or effective buildings. How short-lived is the advantage of a new school facility; how fleeting is the benefit of brand new textbooks; how ephemeral is the life of an innovative program.

Whenever good things occur in a classroom, whenever test scores improve, whenever kids display positive attitudes or excitement in learning, it is because of a teacher, not a program, a building, or a policy.

Whenever good things occur in a classroom it is because of a teacher, not a program, a building, or a policy.

While organizational arrangements such as an academic block under the direction of a team open up opportunities, they don't assure improvement. It is only when the faculty members involved take advantage of the situation, plan and grow professionally together, that improved learning for students results. Even computers, awesome as they are in their educational capability and potential, pale in significance when stacked against the importance of the person of the teacher.

Middle level education stands or falls more nearly on the student-teacher relationship than on any other thing. Teachers spell success, not programs. We who are often the enemy, are also really the only possible conquerors.

So, while not denying the validity of that universal truth expressed by Pogo, perhaps we should also point out that there is a corollary: "We have also met the allies, and he too is us ."

November, 1987

On assumptions, brains, and rubber bands

"It weren't my ignorance that done me in, it was the things I knowed that weren't so."

The above bit of wisdom from literature's Josh Billings is certainly applicable to organized education. So many practices and procedures, long accepted and rarely questioned, continue to direct our educational efforts, yet they are based on invalid or nonexistent rationales. For instance, the belief that approximately 30 students constitute a class still is a basic determinant in planning and building schools, yet that number has little or no learning theory or psychological research to undergird its validity as the proper size for a learning community.

Another thing that is "knowed" but isn't so is the nature of intelligence. For long years it has been assumed that intelligence was inherited and predetermined — some had it and some did not. It was essentially one-dimensional and largely unalterable. The teacher's job was only to discover and nurture that preexistent ability. Much of the plan and structure of education in the United States was built on such a notion about the nature of ability or intelligence.

Ability is many-dimensional, shifting, variable, and subject to development.

We know that in holding such views we may have been wrong, harmfully wrong. Ability, we are discovering, is many-dimensional, shifting, variable, and subject to development. Much of what we call intelligence is learned rather than inherited. There is a heredity component, to be sure. However, heredity does not determine a fixed point, a genetically determined level of intelligence which later, when tested, will become an I.Q. score. Rather heredity only determines a range of potential, and that range might be likened to a rubber band. Experiences will determine how much that band will be stretched. (But rarely, for any of us, to its full extent.)

The teacher's job, under this newer view, is as much a matter of creating the capacity to learn as it is a process of filling a predetermined capacity. Educational efforts should have a multiplier effect as well as an additive effect. What students are taught should not just increase their knowledge but should, in fact, increase their ability to learn. Early adolescents should not be branded with labels that infer a fixed capacity. Rather, we ought to view, in the words of Melvin Tumin, "every child as a set of open possibilities."

The teacher's job is as much a matter of creating the capacity to learn as it is a process of filling a predetermined capacity.

A child's earliest experiences have enduring importance and that importance cannot be overestimated. Yet also of special importance and enduring influence are the experiences young people have as they reach the critical stage of mental development that occurs during the latter part of early adolescence. In many respects, it is a second and last chance to stretch that ability band.

For a rare one or two in the sixth grade, for some in the seventh grade, and for many in the eighth grade, the capacity to think analytically *begins* to emerge. But that ability to think about thinking, to hypothesize, may never be developed if early adolescents are not challenged, enticed, even pushed, to use their full mental capacities.

The mental prowess of our nation's youth is not likely to be exploited adequately if teachers at the middle level do not recognize that the mental capacities of their students are open to expansion and development. If assumptions about "limited ability" become too deeply ingrained expectations remain low — and so does performance. If elementary methods based on concrete operations are perpetuated too long, the critical time to assist pupils in moving into formal operations may be lost. Middle school teachers can, indeed, make a difference in behavior, skills, attitudes — and even in intelligence!

February, 1988

36

A pat on the back

As significant others, middle school teachers deserve support and encouragement. Over the years my work with schools has taken me to many states and places and I've had the privilege of meeting and knowing, however briefly, hundreds of middle level teachers. My role is sometimes as an evaluator, sometimes as a consultant or speaker, sometimes as a staff development instructor or institute staff member, sometimes just as a visitor.

Inevitably, regardless of the role, as one who is supposed to be somewhat knowledgeable I am expected, it seems, to critique, to point out weaknesses, to indicate areas needing improvement, to judge. I'm willing to do this as best I can, but I want to devote this column to express a positive view, to commend a most deserving group — middle level teachers. Their work is praiseworthy and my admiration for them is genuine.

Overall, the level of professionalism, commitment, and conscientious effort is higher among middle level folk than at any other level.

The room for improvement is big — we are all in it — but those serving in our nation's middle level classrooms surely deserve, at the very least, a pat on the back. Some are better than others, a good many operate under wrong assumptions, some lack certain skills, a few would even prefer to be somewhere else, others may have their priorities out of order; but overall, the level of professionalism, commitment, and conscientious effort is, I am convinced, higher among middle level folk than at any other level.

I have observed in a host of schools and classrooms, sat in on team meetings, talked with faculty, both formally and informally. I've interviewed students by the dozens. Out of these experiences comes, first and foremost, genuine respect and admiration for the teachers of early adolescents. Sure, there are failings and flaws — and there always will be for even good teachers are humans — but those who interact daily with volatile young adolescents deserve support and encouragement. They work hard. They are sensitive to individuals, and, with rare exceptions, they treat kids humanely. They seek to be appropriate "significant others" in the lives of their students.

Those who interact daily with volatile young adolescents deserve support and encouragement.

Traditional organizational arrangements and teachers' own needlessly low self concepts often keep them responsible for too many different kids for too short a time and, presumably, for the presentation of just a single subject. Well intended but misplaced pressure forces them to focus too much on the acquisition of isolated information and the testing of its temporary retention. Reporting procedures usually underemphasize the non-academic aspects of middle level education and make teachers feel almost guilty when time is taken to deal with more behaviorally oriented goals.

There is, then, lots of work to be done, but as the school year draws to a close I salute those who work with early adolescents. Well done, committed and caring teachers.

May, 1988

Call the psychiatrist!

"If you really want to change the curriculum, don't call the curriculum director, call the psychiatrist!"

That statement may seem ridiculous or a questionable attempt at humor. Educators, usually suspicious of psychiatrists, may dismiss the affirmation as a mere attention-getter. But put your predispositions aside and think about the element of truth that is contained in the assertion, "If you really want to change the curriculum call for the psychiatrist."

Curriculum change is difficult to achieve. Exciting ideas, logical programs, and research-based instructional procedures abound. The good intentions of boards of education and school administration are conscientiously pursued. Even special incentive funds are often available to implement change. But the status quo yields begrudgingly and very little. Why?

Change efforts do not break down in the boardroom or the curriculum center; they break down at the level of the individual classroom. Curriculum change, inevitably and ultimately, calls for teachers to change. And because teachers are human, they find change frightening. Curriculum change requires teachers who are willing and able to give up the familiar — ones who can deal with possible failure and considerable uncertainty — things which are inherent in one's being and have little to do with technical knowledge.

Curriculum change, inevitably and ultimately, calls for teachers to change and, as humans, teachers find change frightening.

Change in itself is upsetting, even scary. It threatens and puts one at risk. This reality is rather universal. It applies to farmers, merchants, executives, and just about everybody else. The unfamiliar almost always gives rise to a tinge of fear. Change, however, bears especially heavy on teachers because of the tremendous responsibilities they carry and the complex, interactive human environment they preside over. After working out a system of management and control and establishing a pattern of instruction, and after securing student acceptance of the conditions, teachers are naturally hesitant to introduce new elements or conditions that may alter the unwritten contract that has been negotiated with students.

Even when the classroom procedures in force are recognized by the teacher as only partially effective, they nevertheless provide needed security. The maintenance of that security is likely to take precedence over a gamble on an "innovation." Proposed changes are likely to be threatening, so teachers, unconsciously, may begin to defend themselves and develop rationales as to why the new idea won't work. This is not done maliciously, even intentionally, only humanly. The behavior of teachers, as with all humans, is determined more by emotions and attitudes than by intellectual considerations and knowledge. The accuracy of the facts or the validity of the theory rarely determine human behavior.

If you want to change people, you have to be willing to deal with the personal, emotional aspects of human interaction and development.

So if you want to change the curriculum, you have to change people. And if you want to change people, you have to be willing to deal with the personal, emotional aspects of human interaction and development. You have to help people overcome the natural inclination to resist change, to build their personal security and self-esteem, to face feelings — the things that are the psychiatrist's stock in trade.

A non-threatening climate must be created. The ability of teachers to succeed in whatever program is proposed must be demonstrated. The full implications of the change must be illuminated fully and time provided for them to be internalized. Care must be taken to avoid defensive, self-survival reactions which cause people to withdraw. Indications of support must be very evident. Some options should be provided.

The movement away from traditional junior high school practices toward full implementation of the middle school concept demands considerable change in school organization, grouping practices, instructional procedures, even in the role of the teacher and the openly acknowledged responsibilities of the school itself. Such changes cannot be accomplished by alterations in the rules or regulations, or by adopting different curriculum content or courses of study, or by purchasing new textbooks or teaching tools. They can only be accomplished by classroom teachers who are secure, open, self-confident, and fully comfortable with kids and with themselves.

Needed changes can only be accomplished by classroom teachers who are secure, open, self-confident, and fully comfortable with kids and with themselves.

We may not want literally to call in the psychiatrist, but if we expect to make needed changes in the broadly conceived curriculum, we must weigh the impact of change on the human side of the professional and be willing to deal somehow with those personal, emotional aspects of human beings that are fundamental to change.

July, 1988

Just what should every early adolescent know?

This is a question I believe each of us in middle level education must grapple with during the year. The fundamental educational issues that underlie this question are under examination with renewed intensity. Whether we are teachers, counselors, administrators, parents, board members, teacher educators or some variations thereof we must all be philosophically ready to engage in dialogue concerning these issues and be able to influence the consensus that will emerge in the months just ahead.

While it is somewhat trite to say that middle level education is approaching a crossroads, it is an apt statement. The impact of *A Nation At Risk* is still being felt. The obsession over tests and test scores has not abated. Teachers are being inundated with cookbook-like worksheets, lists of objectives to be mastered, and related skill drills. The "cultural illiteracy" of America's youth has been widely proclaimed and publicized.

Fortunately, we also have the Carnegie Corporation's report, *Turning Points: Preparing Youth for Life in the Twenty-first Century.* This publication's recommendations are completely in line with the advocacies of NMSA and its members.

The state of public education is a serious national problem with far-reaching implications.

All of these events point to an impending time of decision in American education. The middle level, currently the site of the most extensive and genuine improvements in education, is going to be at the center of the debate as differing views of what constitutes a good education for American youth vie for support.

I do not question the seriousness of the educational problem. The knowledge deficiencies and incompetencies of many of our youth are frightening. The mounting concern over at-risk adolescent youth is well placed, indeed. The state of public education is a serious national problem with far-reaching implications. Major reforms are called for. I do, however, question some of the proposals being advanced and the assumptions they are based on.

They run counter to my own philosophy and understanding of the middle school concept. The solutions seem to rely on improving the content and insuring the mastery of it. But my own experience indicates that almost all of the desired general content has always been included and was "covered."

Is there a solution?

The solution, as I see it, lies more nearly in improved instructional processes, concern for developing positive attitudes, the functional teaching of skills, and attention to those objectives that go beyond the acquisition of information. It is naive to believe that any real improvement can come from specifying the uniform content that is to be taught without otherwise altering the educational environment.

> *The solution lies more nearly in improved instructional processes, concern for developing positive attitudes, the functional teaching of skills, and attention to those objectives that go beyond the acquisition of information.*

I do not advocate a watering down of the curriculum. I am not willing to accept less rigorous intellectual activity or easy standards; and I do believe that the school has a clear responsibility to share with each new generation our cultural heritage and the accomplishments of the past. I believe, however, we must examine fully some basic issues that are inherent in the question, "What should every early adolescent know?" The related question "How should we organize middle level schools to provide these educational experiences?" deserves equal consideration.

Think on these things

A review of the deep-seated issues contained in these questions and their implications is beyond the scope of this column, so let me simply list some points, stated as queries, that I believe warrant our attention.

—Should the major goal of elementary and middle level schools be to "prepare students for the high school?"

—What will the children born today who will live all of their adult lives in the 21st century need to know?

—Is this statement by John Goodlad valid? "Those who still live in the past confidently set the norms for educating those who will live in the future?"

—Which is more serious, the knowledge gap or the values gap?

—Given the geometric increase in knowledge, science, art, literature, social studies, etc., is it realistic to assume that youth today could still learn all the conventional content that those of us over forty studied and still be able to understand the vast, far-reaching social, scientific and political developments that have occurred in the last thirty years?

—While today's fifteen year olds do not know much that we presumably knew at fifteen, is it not also true that today's fifteen year olds know far more about many things than earlier generations knew at fifteen?

—Is there handwriting on the wall that points to the middle school of the next century, if not the next decade, being skill centered rather than subject centered?

—Are the cultural literacy and content specific proposals compatible with what we know about human growth and development and the developmental nature of early adolescents?

My own answers are rather obvious I suspect, both in the selection and the phrasing of the questions. What are your answers?

January, 1989

Homework — is a new direction needed?

Homework. It has been a part of the formal schooling process as long as anyone can remember. Everybody from the age of six to ninety-six knows what it means. Most parents believe in it. They think, like castor oil, it's good for you.

Across the years homework has been imbued with all sorts of virtues. It teaches responsibility. It even builds "character." It is necessary to practice the lessons presented in school. It leads to better grades. It keeps parents informed about what students are learning. Homework makes possible more efficient use of time in school. And so it goes . . .

Recently it has received renewed support and teachers have been urged to assign additional homework and check it more carefully. Some boards of education have made the assignment of daily homework a requirement. It's all a part of making our nation less "at risk."

Isn't it time to do some soul-searching about homework at the middle level, and to nudge it in a new direction?

To question homework, then, is to put oneself "at risk." But I wonder if it isn't time to do some soul-searching about homework at the middle level, and to nudge it in a new direction. Students dislike homework. When asked what they don't like about school, the most common answer is consistently "homework." They consider it a "pain" and boring. They question its value.

Given the critical importance of student attitudes and the effect they have on performance and behavior, I wonder if we want to perpetuate practices known to evoke such negative views toward school and toward education itself. At a time when youth are ready to explore new vistas and new topics, when they are tired of academic exercises and hunger for real experiences, could not varied out-of-class directed experiences (read: homework) contribute to these goals more than required-of-all busywork? (at least until parents and society in general develop the emphasis on education and personal responsibility that once made quite acceptable the reliance on routine assignments.)

Any claim that research results show increased achievement because of homework won't hold water.

At the elementary level there is value in the routine of regular homework and the habits its use instills. At the middle level, however, the routine use of common homework assignments may not be the way to go. Studies on the effects of homework done over several decades present a mixed bag. Any claim that research results show increased achievement because of homework won't hold water. It makes a difference only when certain conditions are met, conditions that are not present when assignments are made "en masse" to the four or five classes which middle level teachers conduct.

Whenever a single, common assignment is given to a class of middle school students it is a questionable assignment.

"What is everybody's business is nobody's business." This old saw applies to much if not most homework. It is safe to say that, with few exceptions, whenever a single, common assignment is given to a class of middle school students it is a questionable assignment. So often such an assignment results in spending excessive class time trying to determine who, in fact, had done their homework. On occasions, homework becomes the tail that wags the dog — to the detriment of critical thinking and creative activities.

Suggestions for improving assignments

I am not advocating the abolition of out-of-school assignments, far from it. Nor am I suggesting a change just because students don't like homework. (Nor am I denying that a great many middle level teachers handle homework in a proper and effective way.) What I do suggest is that a shift in direction, purpose, and some procedures ought to be

46

instigated. It would be well if we could move homework in such a direction that the perception of it was not busywork, but rather enrichment.

Out of school assignments could be means of fulfilling the important exploratory responsibilities of middle schools rather than reflections of a continued reliance on elementary routines. Assignments could provide some options or alternatives, and even, occasionally, some excitement. They don't have to involve all students in the class every week-night. Homework doesn't have to rely so heavily on textbooks — one study reported that 90% of homework is spent on text materials!

Homework ought to involve parents frequently in a positive, participatory role rather than just a supervisory role. At home the question, "Have you done your homework?" has become a wedge driving the generations further apart. The words themselves are not negative, but the tone in which they are usually spoken makes the question divisive.

Homework ought to involve parents frequently in a positive, participatory role rather than just a supervisory role.

So often we make a lot of assignments but take little time in making them — when we could make fewer assignments but take more time in developing them. Joint assignments involving two or more teachers make sense.

Making assignments very specific for a few students is better than having all students pursue a common assignment. For instance, if Chapter 12 is to be the focus of tomorrow's discussion, instead of assigning all to read the chapter, have each row of students read the material with a limited, but very specific, purpose. For instance, those in one row might each be expected to prepare five or ten good test questions on the chapter. Another row might be asked to identify in the chapter new or difficult words which others might not know and be ready to put them on the board with definitions. A third row might be responsible for developing outlines with a fourth providing supplementary information regarding proper names or characters, and so on. One or two rows might even get the night off. Under such an arrangement, there would be a readiness for attacking that chapter tomorrow that wouldn't exist if all were simply told to read and be ready to discuss or answer the questions at the end of the chapter.

Small group community-based activities are other possibilities. For instance, volunteers could interview certain persons or survey a number of adults on various contemporary issues about which early adolescents are concerned.

The middle school concept is based exclusively on the nature and needs of early adolescents. Its characteristics are all directly related to what is known about the age group. Should not that venerable phase of formal education, homework, also reflect that knowledge? A revolution may not be called for, but, as I see it, evolutionary changes are needed to move homework more in line with the middle school concept.

March, 1989

An assignment
for the summer

When the school year moves toward closure no new approach or activity is likely to be initiated. The patterns of present practices have hardened. Our professional concern for improvement must, then, focus on next year. And while I don't want to burden your well-earned summer R&R needlessly, I want to challenge you to doing some serious contemplation during the coming hiatus from the classroom. My hope is that, come September, you might initiate some sorely needed fundamental changes in the teaching/learning enterprise.

Reform means restructuring

To implement fully the middle school concept will require a modicum of major restructuring, largely growing out of a redefinition of the teacher's role. We need to face the fact that the improvements needed in middle level education cannot be achieved by simply doing better what, for most of us, is now common practice. No fully prescribed curriculum presented by a telling teacher is up to meeting the varied needs of our young adolescents.

The improvements needed in middle level education cannot be achieved by simply doing better what, for most of us, is now common practice.

For decades America's quest for educational improvement has been conscientiously devoted to pouring yards of concrete, purchasing hardware and software, and instituting new and special programs. The clatter and claims of novel approaches have often drowned out the real essence of teaching and learning. We meant well. We did want to build better schools, but somehow in the rash of reforms we have lost something of the wholeness of teaching, something, if you will, of its soul. We sought to improve by instituting innovations and issuing invoices — and success by these means has been limited.

In the rash of reforms we have lost something of the wholeness of teaching, something, if you will, of its soul.

John Dewey understood such an eventuality when he penned these words long ago. "It is our American habit if we find the foundations of our educational structure unsatisfactory to add another story or wing. We find it easier to add a new study or course or kind of school than to reorganize existing conditions so as to meet the need."

More recently, George Leonard criticized the current reform movement by commenting that in a world characterized by major changes in every other aspect of life "the reformers are offering the nation an educational horse and buggy. They would improve the buggy, keep the passengers in it longer, and pay the driver more. But it would still be a horse and buggy. "

There is the danger that the middle school movement will too quickly find satisfaction in a revised grade level structure, in administratively organized teams, and even in established AA programs, and fall short of making the fundamental changes in the teaching/learning complex that are needed to make the most of America's marvelous educational opportunities.

Redefinition of teaching

At the heart of the problem is a perpetuation of a very narrow and largely outdated concept of what teaching is and what it really entails. Most Americans believe, and indeed I suspect most teachers operate pretty much on the notion, that knowledge is static and that learning is assimilation. Neither assumption is false, but both are grossly incomplete. Knowledge is not merely passed on, it evolves and is created. Learning is a matter of active construction not merely retention.

Knowledge is not merely passed on, it evolves and is created. Learning is a matter of active construction not merely retention.

50

The limited, traditional views of teaching and learning have become so ingrained, so institutionalized, that they are rarely questioned. Schools and classrooms have been built and furnished in such a way that these concepts are reinforced. An adversarial relationship between students and teacher is inherent in the physical setting wherein students and teacher face one another. Yet real improvement in middle level education is heavily dependent upon getting the student and the teacher on the same side of the desk!

Real improvement in education is heavily dependent upon getting the student and the teacher on the same side of the desk!

There is now much talk of "restructuring." It is overdue. It has been recognized that the recent top-echelon reforms have met with limited success. The necessity of getting closer to the classroom and the student/teacher relationship if real improvements are to occur has become clear. The middle level school, which is open and forward looking, has a head start and is the school best able to carry out such restructuring.

A summer's assignment

So in the next couple of months do some serious thinking about early adolescents, their needs, educational priorities, the traditional curriculum, and the nature of the teacher's job in the 90s. To advance your thinking read a good book like *In the Middle* by that master eighth grade teacher Nancie Atwell or one of Elliot Wigginton's books. Our commitment to middle level education and its enduring importance calls for a summer's assignment of grappling with our beliefs and philosophy of education — all with the goal of stepping out from the pack as America comes to grips with the need to restructure her schools.

May, 1989

Strike while the iron is hot

Much wisdom is embodied in the old maxims familiar to us all. They have lasted over time and become clichés because they contain truth. And people who have never had either a first or second hand experience with a forge or a hammer and wouldn't know an anvil from an A-frame, understand the message contained in the adage *strike while the iron is hot.*

Success is so often simply a matter of timing, seizing the fleeting opportunity to shape events when conditions are favorable.

Success is so often simply a matter of timing. It is seizing the fleeting opportunity to shape events and being proactive when the conditions are favorable. Teddy Roosevelt once observed that "nine-tenths of wisdom is being wise in time." The junior high school took advantage of that reality and made marked inroads in the established 8-4 plan in the early 1900s because a variety of events and conditions supported the change. So, as I see it, the early years of the last decade of this same century present a comparable time for the middle school.

Supportive conditions exist

Major events and conditions, both in society and the educational establishment, point to the year 1990 as a propitious time for implementing more fully the middle school concept. A growing recognition of the age of early adolescence and its particular significance in setting life's course is evident. So too is the realization that many of the plagues rampant in our society have their starts during these vulnerable years. The rightful concern over that large portion of our students now identified as "at risk" inevitably comes to focus on the middle level years.

The Carnegie Corporation's Task Force report on the middle years has helped to put the spotlight on these years. The report's recommendations coincide beautifully with the long-standing advocacy of active middle school leaders and the NMSA. Subsequently the

Corporation's Foundation has supported follow-up activities in 27 states. Many states already had middle level task forces at work. Evidence from serious research studies is providing guidance and support in the implementation of middle school practices. The existence of so many highly successful middle schools, and the enthusiasm and professionalism so evident among most middle level teachers and administrators provide essential ingredients for positive action.

Can we act?

There is, indeed, good reason to believe that the time is ripe. Yet change in educational practice comes begrudgingly. The hand of tradition is heavy. The pressures on teachers are excessive and sapping, making just survival a nearly full-time job. It will take leadership and courage, along with real commitment, to seize the moment as we should. But can we examine the state of society, our schools, the known needs of early adolescents, contemplate our significant influence, and do less?

We don't know all the answers. On some issues, such as the practice of teaching reading as a separate "subject," there are clear differences of opinion. But on so many basic beliefs about early adolescent education there is almost complete unanimity. We possess that essential ingredient, a shared vision.

Every school containing middle level grades ought to agree on a particular area of improvement and take specific actions in the months ahead.

The middle school, then, is in a good position to move boldly to institute changes known to be needed. Every school containing middle level grades ought to agree on a particular area of improvement and take specific actions in the months ahead. Do not let the weeks slip by till spring fever sets in and dulls all intentions without making some clear move to improve the education being provided early adolescents .

Immediate action options

Although there are many major things that should be accomplished there are also many little things that could be done immediately with minimal effort.

53

While waiting for the larger improvement projects to take shape there are steps individual teachers might take. Let me offer the following suggestions teachers (or an entire faculty) could take.

1. Increase your personal interactions with students. Commit yourself to initiating brief conversations with students whenever possible about anything other than the subject being studied or homework. This has special importance for those pupils who have not experienced much academic success.

2. Provide increased opportunities for students to be actively involved in deciding what they should study and how they might best learn it. Develop the connections between the curriculum and the kids that result in improved motivation.

3. Make the development of critical thinking a goal. Go beyond *who, what, where,* and when to include *why* and *so what.* Even at the risk of covering less content, push students to think, to consider alternatives and implications. The stage of formal operations does not come about automatically. It has to be coaxed and enticed into being.

4. Inform your grade level colleagues of the content, topics, and skills that will be the focus of your class in the immediate future. In no more than one side of a single sheet let those who teach the same youngsters know what you'll be covering so that they can see opportunities to correlate their instruction. (Teams with common planning periods presumably do this routinely .)

We who understand and apply the principle of readiness as we direct classroom activities should not ignore this same principle when it applies in our larger professional life. The educational iron is heated up. The hammer is in your hand. So strike while the iron is hot.

November, 1989

The school as teacher

"We learn what we live, and we learn it to the degree that we live it."
— William Heard Kilpatrick

As educators we spend nearly all of our time, money, and energy dealing with what is taught in the school, with the material that is presented in the various classrooms and courses. We worry, conscientiously, about the content and skills covered in the formal lessons — and, of course, we should. But we spend almost no time dealing with what is taught *by* the school. Yet the school, as an entity, is a powerful teacher, presenting its lessons silently but surely. As middle school educators we need to consider specifically just what the school is teaching via its programs, policies, rules, and regulations, by its "way of life." On analysis, we may be surprised — and chagrined.

The school is not just a physical place in which teachers conduct classes, it is an environment in which youth grow. It is not a teaching factory, but a laboratory of living. The school is not an entity set apart from the rest of society where one learns things needed in a future life; it is life. The ecology of the school, then, as well as its formal curriculum, deserves direct attention.

The school is not a teaching factory, but a laboratory of living.

A discouraging percentage of what is taught explicitly in the formal curriculum is lost in a matter of months, but the lessons that the school teaches implicitly become internalized, subtly but certainly, as students live over time under its tutelage. Students are instructed by the school's behavior.

Much of what students learn from the school as teacher is very positive and desirable, for instance, the clear and well-intentioned provisions by adults of schools for all. However, many lessons are negative and are, in fact, completely contrary to our stated objectives and philosophy. It is important that we become sensitive to the school as teacher and move to rectify those undesirable and unintentional lessons that students are probably learning from life in our schools.

We should be aware of what all is being taught in this hidden curriculum.

Especially during the malleable early adolescent years when youth are raising serious questions and developing their own personal and lifelong answers, we should be aware of what all is being taught in this hidden curriculum.

Some questions to consider

To assist in analyzing what a school may be teaching implicitly the following questions could be examined by the faculty.

• What is taught by the school's grading system? What do students readily conclude are the real objectives of our school? What do we pay off on? Does the grading system even sometimes teach students how to cheat? How does our uniform, single standard grading scale support our purported goal of building positive self-esteem?

How does our uniform, single standard grading scale support our purported goal of building positive self-esteem?

• What lessons are inherent in our discipline codes and policies? Are they based on negative assumptions about the nature of early adolescents? Do they simply specify consequences for assumed misbehavior rather than confirm positive expectations? Do they often encourage kids to learn ways to beat the system? Do students learn, regrettably, the lesson that "adults don't trust us?"

• Does the school's *modus operandi* teach young people compliant behavior, even as we profess to be helping them develop their individuality and initiative?

• Though not our intention, isn't it likely that our tracking and ability grouping practices will teach young people that some of them are worth more than others? What sort of self-concept can be developed by those who spend all day in lower sections?

To influence students' attitudes and beliefs as is necessary, we will have to do more than provide effective instruction in the mandated curriculum.

Particularly if we are serious about helping at-risk youngsters and affecting their out-of-school lives, we must consider what the school itself is teaching. To influence students' attitudes and beliefs as is necessary, we will have to do more than provide effective instruction in the mandated curriculum. We have to teach them with our collective and institutional behavior — for "they learn what they live."

January, 1990

Interdisciplinary teaming— destination or way station?

No single educational idea has come to characterize "the middle school concept" as certainly as has interdisciplinary teaming. It has become almost the *sine qua non* for a real middle school.

Forming interdisciplinary teams is now an acknowledged goal for hundreds of middle level schools. A place of importance for the interdisciplinary team in the middle school movement is, therefore, certain for years to come. It will continue to serve well as an objective for hundreds of schools — including many high schools — seeking to move away from the rigid, departmentalized secondary model and create conditions which do not excessively fragment learning. Since, regrettably, the majority of middle level schools still organize for instruction by single subject departments, it is a most worthy goal.

The merits of interdisciplinary teaming are fairly obvious and have been amply delineated in the literature. I have spoken of them often and have urged their creation where they do not exist. Obviously, then, I am not opposed to interdisciplinary teams, yet I have concerns about their becoming "institutionalized" and being viewed as the destination, the ultimate goal, without regard to their limitations or even their largest possibilities.

Teaming—advantages and limitations

As single subject specialists who were formed in the high school mold took employment in middle level schools their problems of adjustment to the energetic, emotional, and sometimes off-the-wall behavior of young adolescents were significantly alleviated via teams. Teachers on teams could and did focus on the mercurial nature of the students they shared. They provided mutual support. A degree of comradery among students also resulted when students recognized the existence of this learning community because of identity-building activities initiated by the teachers.

Yet moving beyond the level of cooperation in matters of student behavior and routines regarding assignments, tests, and the like has been difficult. It is so easy, so logical, to maintain "turn teaching" when the team is composed of four or five teachers each with an acknowledged subject specialty. The ultimate goal of true interdisciplinary *instruction* has thus been elusive.

The ultimate goal of true interdisciplinary instruction has been elusive.

An occasional thematic unit has provided variety and excitement but the day-in day-out approach has been to pursue an understanding of life and the world's problems through the study of traditional subjects. It is increasingly clear that, to date, organizing faculties into interdisciplinary teams in the vast majority of cases has failed to achieve the interdisciplinary instruction desired.

Teaming has given the teachers involved a needed sense of professionalism and boosted morale, but it has also permitted the subjects to continue as entities, even where the natural correlations may be highlighted. So long as the labels on the teachers and their classes are subjects, bodies of content, predetermined and prescribed, it has been difficult to make the leap to true interdisciplinary instruction and to incorporate the degree of student-teacher planning that is necessary if the curriculum is to become truly student-centered.

At the same time that the academic teachers have elevated their status via teaming, the typical arrangement, rather ironically, has kept the exploratory teachers on the fringe of the school program.

A clear limitation of teams of four or five teachers is that they do little to lessen the long-standing teacher load problem.

Another clear limitation of teams of four or five teachers is that they do little to lessen the long-standing teacher load problem. The personal influence that middle school teachers could have and should have is handicapped by the limited amount of time an individual teacher and student have together. It is impossible to deny the reality that a teacher who spends 50 minutes daily with 120 different youngsters is not in nearly as good a position to know them and influence them, academically and behaviorally, as is a teacher who spends 100 minutes daily with 60 different youngsters or one who spends 150 minutes a day with only 30 youngsters.

So often in a single 45-50 minute period it is possible for both student and teacher to avoid really encountering one another. Genuine interaction is easily bypassed and less than satisfactory personal relations tolerated in a single period class, although the teacher may not consciously seek that condition. When teachers and students stay together for a longer time more satisfactory relationships are worked out — which in itself is a skill needed as young people move toward adulthood.

Likewise, when students and teachers stay together longer with broadened responsibilities, the artificial separation of life and its problems into "subjects" is less likely to occur. In pursuing, for instance, a unit of the problem of garbage and waste disposal, the obvious interrelationships between that problem and social studies, science, mathematics, and other areas will be assets not liabilities as students and teachers plan ways to understand fully this serious issue.

When students and teachers stay together longer with broadened responsibilities, the artificial separation of life and its problems into "subjects" is less likely to occur.

Teaching early adolescents, it has to be recognized, is much more than merely instructing. It is presiding over human growth and development. It is guiding the critical and now accelerated maturation process. To do this most effectively calls for a relationship that is more than perfunctory and passing. The typical interdisciplinary team composed of four or five subject specialists, while taking a giant step toward interrelated instruction and student-focussed learning, may not be in the best position to direct the full education of emerging adolescents.

While continuing to move across the curriculum organization continuum in the right direction, I believe it would be well for us as middle level educators to recognize the establishment of good interdisciplinary teams as a very important way station, but not assume such to be the final destination as we take seriously the charge to restructure our schools.

March, 1990

The middle school — the exploratory school

If the intermediate school in America's educational system were not labelled *middle school* it could well be called *the exploratory school*. The concept of exploration is that central to and universal in the mission of the middle level school. Exploration, properly viewed, is an approach and a point of view that should permeate the entire curriculum as well as being a particular component in the total program.

This is a notion that has been inherent in middle level education for at least 70 years, but was never implemented adequately in the junior high school and, with limited exceptions, is not present in the majority of today's middle schools.

In part this lack of broad programmatic implementation is due to a limited understanding of the concept itself coupled with a limited understanding of the nature of early adolescents. One cannot blame the fathers of the junior high school for failing to articulate the idea of exploration. Thomas Briggs (1920) in his original five functions of the junior high school incorporated the concept in most of the five functions. His list of the purposes of the intermediate school, which became the best known such statement, was as follows:

1. To continue, in so far as it may seem wise and possible, and in a gradually decreasing degree, common, integrating education;

2. To ascertain and reasonably to satisfy pupils' important immediate and assured future needs;

3. To explore, by means of material in itself worthwhile, the interests, aptitudes, and capacities of pupils;

4. To reveal to pupils, by materials otherwise justifiable, the possibilities in the major fields of learning;

This article originally appeared in the Summer 1990 *TAMS Journal*, a publication of the Tennessee Association of Middle Schools.

5. To start each pupil on the career which, as a result of the exploratory courses, he, his parents, and the school are convinced is most likely to be of profit to him and to the investing State (pp. 162-174).

Another of the original junior high school pioneers, Leonard Koos (1920) also identified exploration as a special objective of the proposed school.

In the celebrated *Cardinal Principles of Secondary Education* (1918) in addition to identifying the "Seven Cardinal Principles," the Commission on the Reorganization of Secondary Education spoke specifically about exploration as follows: "In the junior period emphasis should be placed upon the attempt to help the pupil explore his own aptitudes and to make at least provisional choice of the kinds of work to which he shall devote himself" (p.13).

Unfortunately, initiated as a downward extension of secondary education, the junior high became just that adopting almost all of the high school's approaches and programs in the now-claimed seventh and eighth grades. Exploration was relegated to short-term try-out courses that were designed primarily to help pupils make more appropriate choices of electives in the high school. Little was done outside of those usual semester electives to help further the goals of exploration. However, it should be recognized that giving voice to the concept of exploration was a definite contribution of the junior high school.

During the 1940s, the voice of William Gruhn became dominant re: the functions of the junior high school. Gruhn, working with his colleague Harl Douglass (Gruhn & Douglass, 1947), had developed a new statement of functions that continues today as a valid statement for all middle level schools. One of the functions he identified was *exploration*. It was summarized in these statements:

To lead pupils to discover and explore their specialized interests, aptitudes and abilities as a basis for decisions regarding educational opportunities.

To lead pupils to discover and explore their specialized interests, aptitudes and abilities as a basis for present and future vocational decisions.

To stimulate pupils and provide opportunities for them to develop a continually widening range of cultural, social, civic, avocational, and recreational interests (p. 59).

When the middle school concept was being promulgated in the 1960s, exploration took on new life. Efforts to develop middle level programs that more nearly reflected the nature of early adolescents usually incorporated expanded exploratory programs. The required cycle of art, music, home economics, and industrial arts became something of a minimum standard. Experimentation with enrichment mini-courses and activity programs occurred. But the "back to basics" thrust of the 70s brought much experimentation to a halt.

Then, in 1983, when the report *A Nation At Risk* was released and was widely publicized exploratory programs suffered again. Such courses appeared to many who were uninformed about the nature of early adolescents to be expendable. Increased attention to the basics and to higher academic standards cut into exploratory programs.

But now the 1990s have begun and a new, brighter era of development in middle level education is underway. The release of *Turning Points* by the Carnegie Corporation in 1989 combined with the leadership of NMSA, its 37 affiliates, NASSP, and other national organizations focussing on the middle level has set the stage for what I believe will be a decade of development.

As the public's and the profession's understanding of early adolescence increases and as the spotlight of attention illuminates the middle level school, the exploratory function will surely benefit. Serious examination of the nature of young adolescents will inevitably lead to the conclusion that the exploratory component of the curriculum is the one component that most directly and fully reflects the nature and needs of this age group. It is clear as well that an exploratory approach should be used in all aspects of the curriculum for, by nature, young adolescents are adventuresome, curious explorers.

The exploratory component of the curriculum is the one component that most directly and fully reflects the nature and needs of this age group.

There is a particularly critical side to this exploratory responsibility of the middle level school, for, in many respects, it is a last chance. If youth pass through the age of early adolescence without broad exploratory experiences their future lives may be needlessly restricted, for it is during this period of development that youth needs to experiment, to ascertain their special interests and aptitudes, to get a broad view of life and the world.

As an individual young adolescent answers the all-important question, "Who am I?" he ought to be able to say, for instance, that the orderliness of bookkeeping procedures has an appeal for me. For many, exploratory courses will be the last chance to sample the world of knowledge before they become committed to a particular program track in the high school. They need the chance to experience music, though never destined to be a musician, to have a part in a play, though never to be an actor, to dabble in crafts though never to be a craftsman.

For many, exploratory courses will be the last chance to sample the world of knowledge before they become committed to a particular program track in the high school.

While exploration, as noted above, is not a new responsibility of the middle level school, the concept itself has expanded considerably as have the means of implementing it. Special exploratory experiences are now viewed as having value in and of themselves, regardless of any value in selecting future studies or vocational pursuits. Unfortunately, the place of the exploratory responsibility in other aspects of the curriculum has not been recognized sufficiently. All too often a regrettable dichotomy has developed between the academics and the exploratories. Sometimes exploratory teachers feel like second class citizens, despite the fact that it is in the exploratories that the best examples of effective middle level teaching are most often found.

Middle schools seeking to implement fully the concepts advocated will have to examine their total programs carefully to determine how the exploratory responsibility can be met more fully through the guidance program, student activities, the academic block, the exploratory courses themselves, and in other aspects of school life.

Components of a broad exploratory program

Since exploration is an attitude and a general approach as well as specific content it is inappropriate to divide it up. But for purposes of adequate explanation the following six components of a full exploratory program for a middle level school can be identified.

1. **The required cycle for general exploratory experiences.** This cycle most typically includes art, music, home economics, and industrial arts. Foreign language, general business, computers, and speech are other areas frequently provided. Six, nine, or twelve week durations for these courses are all possibilities.

2. **Electives.** Usually following required exploratory experiences, semester or full-year electives are a second element in a comprehensive exploratory program. These would provide an opportunity to pursue at a higher grade level an area that had appeal. For instance, following a required nine weeks experience in art in the seventh grade, a semester elective in drawing and painting might be offered in the eighth grade.

3. **Interest-centered mini-courses** comprise a third component. They may be both academically and recreationally oriented, but exist for enrichment and exploration rather than for mastery. Almost any faculty hobby or student interest can be the focus of these short-term experiences. They may run the gamut from guitar playing to rocket building, from fun with a hand calculator to knitting.

These variable exploratory experiences, usually offered in a 25-35 minute period for 12 to 18 meetings, do not have to have academic legitimacy and ought not to be graded in any way which seeks to reflect levels of achievement. There is no pattern of desirable or "right" mini-courses; they can be as diverse as human interest and creative talent make them. Parents and community adults can be utilized as co-teachers in these experiences. The opportunity to pursue an interest with like-minded peers and a caring adult is the key as much as the content itself. Though many would consider such classes as "frills," they are very basic and valid.

4. **Independent study,** though often overlooked, is an excellent means of fulfilling the exploratory responsibility. Somehow it seems to have been assumed that only gifted students can learn independently, when, in fact, average and below average students are often assisted by, and quite competent in learning on an independent basis. Independent study can be an outgrowth of work within the academic block or a part of separate enrichment experiences.

5. **Clubs, organizations, and assemblies** provide abundant opportunities for engaging in experiences that are new, broadening, and enjoyable. These student activities, which include student government, offer opportunities for leadership, citizenship training, and meaningful service — all especially significant matters at this level of human development. At the middle level, such activities certainly should not be referred to as *extra-curricular*. To the students, they almost always provide the school experiences remembered longest and best.

6. **An exploratory approach in teaching all subjects,** while not an entity or a distinct component, is really the foundational means of fulfilling the exploratory responsibility. In fact, nearly everything done in a middle level school should be done in an exploratory mode, for, as stated in the opening paragraph, the middle school is the exploratory school. One should teach language arts, for instance, with an exploratory view, as literature is sampled and many opportunities for applying the skill of reading both for securing knowledge and for recreation are provided.

Such an exploratory viewpoint can do much to bring about the marriage of the often-estranged couple, academics and exploratories. There is no standard or right way to organize an exploratory program or to determine its content. It, like the kids it serves, is variable. But, however a school decides to fulfill this central mission of the middle level it deserves as much time and attention as any other aspect of the program. While the spotlight is usually put on the academic block, it may be the adequacy of fulfilling its exploratory function that really determines the success of a middle school.

References

Briggs, T.H. (1920). *The Junior High School.* Boston: Houghton Mifflin Company.

Commission on the Reorganization of Secondary Education (1918). *Cardinal Principles of Secondary Education,* Bulletin 1918, No 35. Washington: U. S. Department of the Interior, Bureau of Education.

Gruhn, W. T. and Douglass, H.R. (1947). *The Modern Junior High School.* New York: The Ronald Press.

Koos, L. V. (1920). *The Junior High School.* New York: Harcourt, Brace, and Howe.

Middle level education: progress, problems, and promises

Eighty years ago the idea of a junior high school was not yet clearly formed. Seventy years ago it was just an infrequent experiment. Sixty years ago the junior high school was the coming thing in American education. Fifty years ago it had achieved considerable status and become a regular part of our educational system. The typical student in the 1940s now went through a school system organized in some way other than the older 8-4, usually a 6-3-3. Forty years ago criticism concerning the junior high school began to mount. Most frequently cited was its tendency to merely mimic the high school in program and policies, to be simply a downward extension of secondary education.

Thirty years ago the middle school, composed of grades 6-8 or sometimes 5-8, was being touted as an alternative and a solution to the failures of the junior high school. Twenty years ago the first comparative studies and surveys revealed that new middle schools and old junior high schools were surprisingly alike in actual practice.

The first comparative studies and surveys revealed that new middle schools and old junior high schools were surprisingly alike in actual practice.

Changes made had been restricted largely to the names of the schools and the grades they contained. Ten years ago, after many needless rounds in the literature of junior high *vs* middle school, junior high and middle school proponents and practitioners began to coalesce into a single cause — the cause of improving early adolescent education.

This article first appeared in the Winter 1990 edition of *Educational Horizons*, published by Pi Lambda Theta.

Today, the phrase middle level education has gained acceptance as the best term to refer to a distinctive level in the continuum of public education however it may be housed in a particular school district.

That, in short, is the history of the movement to reorganize public education. Of course, there is much more to what is the longest-running, most extensive educational reform movement in the United States. This article will touch on many aspects of this most important, but often overlooked, educational development.

PERSPECTIVES

Rooted in human growth and development

The middle level education movement is firmly anchored in the realities of human growth and development. Every specific practice advocated by its leaders is directly related to and compatible with the nature and needs of this special age level. Although early practice in educational administration quickly established the notion that schooling was composed of two levels, elementary for children and secondary for adolescents, youth could not be so arbitrarily and neatly divided.

Although early practice in educational administration quickly established the notion that schooling was composed of two levels, elementary for children and secondary for adolescents, youth could not be so arbitrarily and neatly divided.

The facts of human development make it evident that there is a clear period of transition between childhood and adolescence. For some youngsters this transition period may be compressed into about two years, while for others it is spread out over four or more years. For a good many girls the puberty growth cycle begins in the fifth grade. For a few boys puberty is still ongoing in the ninth grade. But for the vast majority the transition is largely contained in the period bounded by grades, six, seven, and eight. These, then, have become the preferred grades for a middle level school when possible. However, a real middle school has little to do with grade organization *per se*, and youth of ages 10 or 11 to 14 or 15 are young adolescents wherever they are housed and should be programmed accordingly.

Young adolescents are distinguished by their diversity. Though they all go through the "perils of puberty" they start at different times and proceed at greatly varying rates. One seventh grade girl may still play with dolls while another is a mother. One boy may be under five feet tall while a classmate has already risen beyond six feet in height. No other group of grades encompasses so diverse a population. The need to serve diversity is a fundamental and a rather distinctive responsibility of a middle level school.

Not only are there the obvious differences in physical development, but there are comparable differences in social, emotional, and intellectual development. And these other areas of development also assume high priorities in the lives of young adolescents and affect greatly their roles as learners. Their social development, particularly, becomes a matter of great concern and usually takes precedence over other aspects of their lives.

Of special importance

Any attempt to gain a fair perspective on middle level education must include a statement concerning the critical, enduring consequences of the educational experiences youth receive during these years. Early adolescence is more than a transition to other major stages of life. It is, in fact, probably the most crucial period of life. While the senior high school is usually accorded special status and much public recognition, the middle school is the more important educational institution.

These are the years "in which the lines of character are graven." — Alfred North Whitehead

---

These generalizations are true because it is during these middle years that young people form their own answers to the fundamental questions of life and decide on the values and standards which largely determine their behavior in the future. As Alfred North Whitehead phrased it, these are the years "in which the lines of character are graven." Adolescents, like adults, lack pliability, but young adolescents are malleable, impressionable. And teachers, as well as parents, become the models or significant others as these youths seek to answer that fundamental question, "Who am I?"

A full understanding of the nature of young adolescents and a careful analysis of the diverse responsibilities of the school during these years leads inevitably to the conclusion that the middle level school has a more demanding set of tasks to address than schools at any other level.

Lack of identity may be ending

Despite its educational importance, the middle school of grades 6-8 has suffered from a lack of identity as did its predecessor, the 7-9 junior high school. That an intermediate unit *does* exist cannot be questioned; it has been a part of *majority* practice for nearly half a century; and some twelve thousand separate junior highs, intermediate, and middle schools now exist. However, state departments of education, the U.S. Department of Education, textbook publishers, teacher education institutions, and the general public continue virtually to ignore the middle level and, instead, regard public education in just the two older categories, elementary and secondary.

One reason this age level is often overlooked is the lack of a single word to identify this period. Educators have had to use nouns and adjectives in combination — young adolescents, emerging adolescents, late childhood, early adolescents — or coined words — transescents and "tweeners" — to label these youngsters.

The year 1989 may come to be regarded as the landmark year when middle level education came of age.

The year 1989, however, may come to be regarded as the landmark year when middle level education came of age. There is increasing evidence that early adolescent education may have finally crept into public consciousness. The 1989 report of the Carnegie Corporation's task Force on Education of Young Adolescents, *Turning Points: Preparing American Youth for the 21st Century*, is a factor. [1] This major document minced no words in detailing the serious plight of young adolescents in the United States and the all-too-common failures of most middle level schools in attempting to provide programs that correlate with the known needs of this critically important age group. The extensive publicity given the report, due largely to the prestige of its sponsoring organization, may have put the middle grades on the public agenda. The report's recommendations, it should be noted, match almost exactly the long-standing advocacy of active middle level educators and, therefore, they quickly garnered the endorsement of organizations and individuals involved in the movement.

Nineteen eighty-nine could also be identified as the year that the National Middle School Association reached maturity and became a major factor in influencing educational policy. Its growth in membership and in its thirty-nine affiliates, publications, and services has been sure and steady, and its 1989 budget exceeded a million dollars for the first time. Its annual conference in Toronto, Canada, October, 1989 registered over eight thousand educators.

The occasion of National Middle Level Education Week in March 1989 also did much to draw the attention of parents and citizens all across our land to schools serving young adolescents. First initiated in 1987, this activity reached extensive grass roots proportions in 1989. Thousands upon thousands were entertained and informed by students and teachers through a host of local activities and events sponsored by middle level schools.

Television has even lent a hand in promoting the middle level years. The American Broadcasting Corporation led the way with its excellent program, "Wonder Years," featuring the outstanding young adolescent actor, Fred Savage. And the National Broadcasting Corporation's "USA Today" produced a series of brief features on the "In-Between Years." Public television contributed significantly by scheduling the hard-hitting, dramatic series, "DeGrassi Junior High School," during the last few years.

Middle level educators seem to reflect the energy and exuberance which characterize the young adolescents they teach.

Many have noted the infectious enthusiasm, real professional zeal, and the uncommon commitment that is exhibited by middle level educators. This spirit is evident in professional literature, staff development activities, conferences, and national conventions. Middle level educators somehow seem to reflect the energy and exuberance which characterize the young adolescents they teach. The middle school, from all appearances, is an idea whose time has finally come.

Progress in implementing the desired characteristics of middle schools has been documented.[2,3] Growing numbers of schools are instituting interdisciplinary instruction, teacher-based guidance programs, and broad exploratory experiences as they seek to reflect in their current curricula the nature and needs of the students.

The middle school concept is still more promise than practice.

Yet, despite the facts documenting growth in numbers and in characteristics implemented, there is so much yet to be done. The middle school concept is still more promise than practice. The advocated features are still not found in the majority of middle level schools.

PROBLEMS

A number of conditions exist which must be alleviated if the middle school concept is to be put into full operation. Neither theoretical validity nor rhetorical advocacy will suffice unless changes occur in the following conditions:

1. **The general public lacks adequate understanding about and appreciation for the age of early adolescence.** Despite its critical importance, Americans are rather ignorant concerning youth between the ages of approximately ten to fifteen. What perceptions exist are largely negative. Parents seem unable to view their emerging adolescents except in reference to what they were ("What happened to my child?") or what they will be ("Why doesn't she grow up?"). All too often they are insensitive to the real trauma that young adolescents go through as they deal with the most complex set of developmental tasks that life presents. Only when parents understand what is happening to their youngsters and the life-long effects of these occurrences will they support, as they should, such things as full exploratory programs and planned affective education experiences.

2. **The societal context in which education is provided today is particularly complex, heavily negative, highly visible, and largely non-supportive.** Society's problems increasingly are students' problems. Poverty, drug abuse, crime, fractured families — all these have become major handicaps to the education of youth. A significant percentage of school-age children carry burdens far heavier than children ought to be saddled with. Almost daily new reports detail the increasing

incidences of child abuse, the plight of teenage mothers, the scourge of drugs, and the rise in violent homicides. Our society has been characterized well by Beane and Lipka in these sentences:

> We live in troublesome times. Ours is a world of ambiguity and ambivalence, of discontinuity and disbelief. The old order is breaking up not only in the industrial to post-industrial economic shift, but in the lifestyles we choose and the diversity of values we espouse. A quick glance around shows us that many adults are having a hard time finding anything to hang onto. For the young, whose life skills are not so mature, the scenario is even more complicated. Traditional sources of stability such as family, the church, the legal system, and even the prospects for eventual employment are rapidly shifting. The only certainty is uncertainty.[4]

Personal gratification and unbridled consumption are advocated on every hand, while education is attacked. The values prevalent in society do little to encourage students to take their education seriously, let alone sacrificially as was once the case. Young adolescents also suffer from "rolelessness" in today's society. They do not have reasonably active, productive roles to fill in the home, community, and, regrettably, even in the school. This is especially distressing since they are facing the all-important task of forming their identities and self-concepts. Their opportunities for interactions with adults, even parents, have been decreasing for years and are now at a frighteningly low level.

Young adolescents also suffer from "rolelessness" in today's society. They do not have reasonably active, productive roles to fill in the home, community, and, regrettably, even in the school.

---

3. The role of the teacher in the middle years needs to be redefined. To implement fully the middle level concept will require some major restructuring of the task of the teacher. Simply doing better at what is now common practice will not suffice in the 1990s as a means of meeting the needs of young adolescents. No canned curriculum presented by a telling teacher will do the job.

Unfortunately, the limited, traditional views of teaching and learning have become so ingrained that they are seldom questioned. Indeed, they have become institutionalized in the buildings and furnishings wherein students and teachers face one another in an implied adversarial relationship. Yet, the creation of the needed sense of a learning community calls for getting the student and the teacher on the same side of the desk. Teachers need to become coaches, even students, while students need to become more nearly teachers.

Teachers need to become coaches, even students, while students need to become more nearly teachers.

Teachers should be helping students build their own agendas for learning rather than simply imposing theirs — or the Board of Education's. As George Bernard Shaw phrased this idea, "What we want to see is the child in the pursuit of knowledge, and not knowledge in pursuit of the child." At this age of heightened curiosity and genuine eagerness to understand life in all of its manifestations, schools too often restrict their learning activities to textbooks focussed on the past — the then and there — when young adolescents live very much in the present — the here and now.

Unfortunately, middle level schools are caught on the horns of a dilemma on this issue. They face the pressures of national reports and legislative actions which focus almost exclusively on the cognitive domain, while growing research makes it clear that the needs of young adolescents are grounded in the affective domain. While demands for increased achievement and higher test scores are being heard on the one hand, educators sensitive to the nature of young adolescents, on the other hand, are trying to respond with programs that support the nonacademic and more immediate aspects of their total development.

It is not that the middle level school seeks to shrug off any of its basic responsibilities to equip students with information but, rather, that it recognizes the education of young adolescents cannot be divided out and dealt with separately. The National Association of Secondary School Principals' Council on Middle Level Education stated this reality recently in *Middle Level Education's Responsibility for Intellectual Development*.

The recognition that intellectual development is part of broad functions is a hallmark of middle level education that has evolved from the junior high school through the middle school to the middle level education movement. It is grounded in the reality that the nurture(ance) and education of young adolescents must be an integrated venture; physical, social, emotional, and intellectual development are each inexorably woven together in the fabric of early adolescent life.[5]

Citizens and educators must come to recognize that at the early adolescent level there is no conflict between academic effectiveness and developmental responsiveness. Rather the former can be achieved most effectively when the latter is attended to overtly.

Concern over the deficiencies of youth in the knowledge they possess is very valid, but the real crisis in education and American life goes much deeper.

While concern over the deficiencies of youth in the knowledge they possess is very valid, the real crisis in education and American life goes much deeper than is revealed by test scores.

4. The place and the value of curriculum content must be re-examined and realistically assessed. The content of the curriculum, the facts and information presented and tested on, is not nearly as important as it is made out to be. Further, the teaching of it in traditional ways is quite inefficient.

Information, like fish, doesn't keep. The need to re-teach something presumably learned last year is a familiar situation to all who teach. It is far more important that young people be able to solve problems, to think creatively, and to behave responsibly than it is to perform well on paper and pencil tests calling for the temporary retention of information.

5. The development of attitudes, character, and values must become priority items on the educational agenda of middle schools. As John Ruskin claimed long ago, "Education does not mean teaching people to know what they do not know, it means teaching them to behave as they do not behave." The ultimate objective of education lies in behavior, and behavior is attitude driven rather than information driven. Middle schools especially must be openly concerned with the attitudes and values young people are developing. Helping young adolescents to develop positive and humane philosophies of life and standards of behavior has to be a basic responsibility of middle level education.

Helping young adolescents to develop positive and humane philosophies of life and standards of behavior has to be a basic responsibility of middle level education.

Helping individuals to have reasonable and positive views of themselves *as learners* is a part of this task, for their success in future schooling is largely determined by the attitude they develop concerning themselves as learners. Beane and Lipka in their research have concluded that self-concept as a learner accounts for up to 50 percent of school achievement, while ability accounts for, at most, 25 percent of such achievement.[6] Unfortunately, although unintentionally, the practices of formal education lead too many youngsters to conclude they are "dumb" when they may simply be uninformed.

6. **The development of all the communication skills must become a school-wide priority.** Skills, like attitudes, persist after specific information is forgotten. Indeed, the only individual who knows enough is that one who knows how to learn. Given the extent of change and the creation of knowledge in contemporary society, that generalization has never been more valid. The idea is old, however, for Elbert Hubbard long ago pointed out that "the job of the teacher is to make himself unnecessary."

The only individual who knows enough is that one who knows how to learn.

The curriculum-wide attack on the skills that are needed, however, is not the narrow reading/grammar-based approach so often evident. The inability to articulate ideas or express opinions is more of a problem than incorrect grammar or poor spelling. The centrality of language in all of formal education must be recognized and positively exploited. Students learn English best by using it, not by studying it. Therefore, teachers of all subjects should be active in presenting functional opportunities to use language in the pursuit of meaningful educational experiences.

The power of language — written and spoken — needs to be possessed to a reasonable degree by all adult citizens in a democracy. It gives them access to the general knowledge that undergirds our society. It permits the pursuit of personal interests and vocational specialities. It ensures the informed and responsible citizens so desperately needed in our society.

7. **Teacher education and certification must be altered to facilitate the preparation of personnel for middle level schools.** One of the early handicaps to the development of appropriate junior high schools was the lack of teachers trained for this level of teaching. Unfortunately, this handicap has continued to exist. Though progress has been made, it is all too slow, and the need to rely heavily on teachers trained for high school teaching in a single subject has been a major roadblock to implementing school programs designed for young adolescents.[7]

For teachers to be effective at this level they must understand this age group and the sometimes bizarre behavior these kids may exhibit. They also need to be able to provide the support and guidance these youngsters need in their psycho-social development. They need, as well, to be able to employ methods that match the mercurial nature of young adolescents. Teacher preparation programs focussed on early childhood education or high school education simply cannot provide appropriate preparation.

PROSPECTS

There are other conditions that could well be cited. The seven enumerated above, however, cover the bulk of the major problems which handicap the advancement of middle level education. Correcting these conditions will take extensive and continuous efforts by hundreds and hundreds of school faculties, administrators, supervisors, state department personnel, and college teacher educators over many years. The hand of tradition is heavy. The educational bureaucracy is almost self-perpetuating. The call for change arouses apprehension, even fear, in the hearts of teachers who are secure in their established routines. However, the critical importance of middle level education demands that efforts be extended. The long-term welfare of our society is so closely tied up in early adolescent education that to do less is unconscionable.

The hand of tradition is heavy. The educational bureaucracy is almost self-perpetuating. The call for change arouses apprehension, even fear, in the hearts of teachers who are secure in their established routines.

While a clear consensus about the basic characteristics of middle level education has been achieved, the movement is still evolving and all the right answers are not yet in. Middle level schools, then, should remain open. They will need to maintain a focus on the kids rather than on school organization or specific programs. There is always the danger that a school will begin to invest special value in some particular arrangement or program and come to view its implementation as the real goal rather than the improved behavior of youth. Too quickly we become doctrinaire proponents of a project, a program, or some curricular entity and, in effect, impose it on kids.

On the other hand, there is the greater likelihood that we will continue to put too much credence in traditional ways of organizing and teaching, and spend our energies making only minor adjustments that fail to get at the root of the problem.

Despite the magnitude of the tasks faced and despite the realization that change comes begrudgingly, I believe the long-term prospects for the implementation of the middle school concept have to be good. Since the concept is based exclusively on the known facts of human development and the principles of learning, its success would seem certain. Further, the goals of middle level education are completely compatible with the tenets of American democracy. So, with both Mother Nature and Uncle Sam on its side, the likelihood of the ultimate implementation of the middle school concept must be bright.

REFERENCES

1. Carnegie Council on Adolescent Development, *Turning Points: Preparing American Youth for the 21st Century: A Report of the Task Force on Education of Young Adolescents* (Washington, DC: Carnegie Council on Adolescent Development, 1989).

2. P. George and L. Oldaker, *Evidence for the Middle School* (Columbus, OH: National Middle School Association, 1985)

3. W. Alexander and C. K. McEwin, *Schools in the Middle: Status and Progress* (Columbus, OH: National Middle School Association, 1987).

4. J. A. Beane and R. P. Lipka, *When the Kids Come First: Enhancing Self-Esteem* (Columbus, OH: National Middle School Association, 1987), p. 5.

5. Council on Middle Level Education, *Middle Level Education's Responsibilities for Intellectual Development* (Reston, VA: National Association of Secondary School Principals, 1989), p. 1.

6. J. A. Beane and R. P. Lipka, *Self-Concept, Self-Esteem, and the Curriculum* (New York: Teacher's College Press, Columbia University, 1986).

7. W. Alexander and C. K. McEwin, *Preparing to Teach at the Middle Level* (Columbus, OH: National Middle School Association, 1988).

What values are we teaching, should we teach, at the middle level?

What paradoxes humans present: persons and instruments orbiting the earth, yet war in the Middle East, a wall still in Berlin, ghettos in every major city. Food is stockpiled, yet millions are dying of hunger. Man has learned how to swim through the water like a fish; he has learned how to fly through the air like a bird; he has even learned how to traverse outer space as has no known creature, yet he still struggles to walk the earth like a man.

Educational excellence and the three Rs

But even if the condition of mankind is paradoxical, a mixture of pluses and minuses, those of us with open eyes and open hearts cannot rest comfortably with things as they are. As educators we should and must pursue excellence.

"Excellence" — the educational buzzword of the '80s. It has been bandied about loosely and all too frequently. It sounds good, with an aura of righteousness about it, and is so universal in its appeal as to be nearly noncontroversial. Yet what does it really mean? Like "quality education," which it seemed to replace, it can mean almost anything a user wants. It is so rhetorical and is used to justify everything from narrowly conceived compensatory education to enrichment through the humanities.

Most commonly, of course, *excellence* is used as a label for efforts to raise educational standards, increase academic achievement, and improve the level of our youth's skills. I'm for such goals, although I usually disagree with the methods recommended for achieving them. In fact, I sincerely worry over what I see happening as a result of the reactions to the rash of educational critiques released in recent years.

This article is a slightly edited version of a speech presented at a National Association of Secondary School Principals' Conference in San Francisco and subsequently published as NASSP's May 1987 *Schools in the Middle*.

Certainly I have no argument with the goal of the school reform movement. I devote all my efforts to school improvement. Schools, as good as they may be, are obviously not good enough.

Every newscast on radio and TV and every daily paper provides additional examples of the reality that vast numbers of young people, students in or graduates of our schools, are not able to deal properly with the many problems and varied decisions that all teenagers and adults are called upon to make in this day and time.

Vast numbers of young people are not able to deal properly with the many problems and varied decisions that all are called upon to make today.

Inability to cope, to relate, to deal with one's own emotions, to assume personal responsibility, to find satisfaction and meaning in life lead to drug abuse, the excessive consumption of alcohol, violence, crime, child abuse, and suicide, to mention the more obvious of the inappropriate ways of meeting the demands inherent in contemporary life.

But while I agree that schools need improving and I, too, cry out for excellence, I disagree with the methods and recommendations advanced by many lay reformers and even with the responses of many professional educators. This is especially true when the efforts focus on the middle level.

A fetish over the 3 Rs narrowly conceived, leads to naive, simplistic reform efforts. Improper definitions of the academics and excellence have led to distorted views of what is really important and what the education of early adolescents is all about.

There is danger that the reform movement will do serious damage to middle level education — a case of the cure being worse than the disease. We could move from middle schools that demand too little to what amounts to *scholastic reform schools*.

Sincere concern over the seriously deficient skill levels of so many young people often leads boards of education and other well-meaning groups to back the most readily available and seemingly logical solutions. Such solutions are seldom effective. Negative attitudes toward youth in general and minority youth in particular, I regret to say, sometimes seem hidden in the demands for excellence.

There is danger that reforms will do serious damage to middle level education. We could move from schools that demand too little to scholastic reform schools.

Requirements, repetition, and *rigidity,* which may become the new 3 Rs, could create insurmountable barriers that will almost guarantee failure for many whose need for education is greatest.

We do need higher expectations, to be sure, and I call regularly for a pervasive school climate of high expectations. We do need standards, but they must be supported by the means of achieving them. We must guard against the possibility of turning our schools into institutions that perpetuate poverty rather than being the means of moving out of it.

For the lower third of our students, the typical reform recommendations are largely invalid. This significant segment, now often called the "at-risk" students, is a growing group. The rate of dropouts in many states has increased in the last five years, and will likely continue to increase as get-tough reforms are instituted at the very time when demography and sociology are presenting schools with an increased number of students who are poor and ill-prepared for traditional formal schooling.

Excellence in ethics

There is an area of education that is of the greatest importance and ought to have the label of excellence attached to it as well, an area that is more basic than the basics — ethics.

Excellence in ethics is the most needed priority in American education today. The cries for excellence in academic proficiency heard

---

Excellence in ethics is the most needed priority in American education today.

---

at every hand should be applied with the same vigor and intensity to the ultimate arena of human existence, to excellence in ethics.

While the deficiencies of our youth in the basic skills are real and deserve a frontal attack of the first magnitude, values are more basic than the basics. We could, I fear, win the battle of skill development but lose the war of civilized life. Consider this proposition. Suppose by noble and intensive efforts, as well as by many minor miracles, every youngster in America was brought up to grade level in reading by the first of June. What effect would this monumental achievement have on America and the problems that plague her? Very little.

Our contemporary culture is blighted seriously in so many ways, ways that involve young people — even middle schoolers: crime, suicide, drug use and abuse, run-aways, vandalism, fraud, deceit, unbridled selfishness, pessimism, alienation, loneliness, permissiveness.

Despite our wealth and technological expertise, despite our heavy spending in education and social services, crime, especially juvenile crime, is increasing and domestic violence ending in death is a daily occurrence in every major city. Any newspaper provides a litany of social ills that are only tangentially related to the skill levels of the perpetrators. The causes of aberrant behavior lie in other areas.

America's skill ills are not nearly as serious as her moral leukemia.

America's skill ills are not nearly as serious as her moral leukemia. Moral responsibility is the oldest basic of all in this country. Though shared by the home, the church, and the community, civic ethics, fundamental values, and character development are the business of middle level schools. And the good news is that accumulating research shows the greatest academic and skill achievement at the middle level comes when schools directly concern themselves with attitudes, personal development, and socialization.

Education is a moral enterprise and middle school teaching is inherently a matter of morality. It cannot be otherwise, for all human behavior involves valuing. It is not a matter of whether we should teach values or not, but rather a matter of what values are we teaching.

Values education at the middle level

The key question, then, is *what values are we teaching?* What values are self-evident to pupils? Who are our heroes? What do we honor? What values are implicit in our operational policies and procedures? What values are taught by what we don't teach, as well as by what we try to teach?

These are questions that call for serious soul-searching. We do have to be careful because our values are showing. Indeed, they are not just showing, they are being learned! And when we face this reality we may be a bit embarrassed. Though not done intentionally, in most of our schools we are teaching implicitly some things that conflict with our explicit goals and stated purposes.

Although not done intentionally, we teach implicitly things that conflict with our explicit goals.

Consider, for example, what values are inherent in our grading systems. What do our tests say the real objectives of our schools are? What do students soon learn really counts? Do our grading systems support our goal of building positive self-esteem? Does the reporting system correlate well with the broad objectives our public statements say we are concerned about?

What about our discipline codes? What values are inherent in them? Are they based on negative assumptions about the nature of early adolescents? Do they simply specify consequences for assumed misbehavior rather than confirm positive expectations? Do they encourage kids to learn how to beat the system and how to cope with the bureaucracy?

Does our excessive reliance on extrinsic motivation devices dull youth toward knowing the true joy of learning and lead toward developing "reward junkies"? Do our procedures, regulations, and demands teach young people compliant behavior even as we profess to be seeking individualization and initiative?

Do the ways we teach young people in school present learning as a very literal thing? Is the single right answer overemphasized to the detriment of creative thinking?

Do our grouping practices teach young people that some of them are worth more than others? Consider what lessons are ingrained in that youngster who spends all day in the lowest sections. What sort of self-concept can be developed in such circumstances?

Do our grouping practices teach young people that some of them are worth more than others?

What do students learn about our values from the almost nonexistent voice they usually have in developing the rules under which they live in school?

The old aphorism, "What you do speaks so loud I cannot hear what you say," continues to be valid. The moral education that we really teach comes from our behavior, not our words. The lessons of most importance to early adolescents have little relationship to "education" as it is conceived by most adults. The curriculum of climate may be more influential and important than the curriculum of content. They may not remember what we teach them, but they'll remember how we treat them.

The curriculum of climate may be more influential and important than the curriculum of content.

When in class and "on stage" teaching, what pupils are learning may not coincide with the planned lesson. Their eyes may be on us but their minds may be miles away. They are as likely to be assessing our clothing, our complexion, our candor, or our character as the content we are presenting. They may be dreaming about what they would like to be, or deeply engrossed in rehearsing the one-liner they would deliver to the cute girl they pass in the hall between classes.

It is not always easy to know just what they are thinking. Early adolescents, kaleidoscopic kids — they can keep you young or age you quickly. It is a time of life when youth is stranger than fiction.

85

> *Middle schools must recognize how incomplete is their teaching of the advertised curriculum and how influential is their teaching of the hidden curriculum.*

Middle schools must recognize how incomplete is their teaching of the advertised curriculum and how influential is their teaching of the hidden curriculum.

Improving students — improving schools

What pupils become is what they have been taught to become — not formally taught, perhaps, but what they have learned from the examples of adults. If our youth are irresponsible, as often charged, it is because the examples of adults led them to that posture. They weren't born that way. As Maureen Applegate phrased it so beautifully and simply many years ago: "Children of all nations are alike, until adults teach them."

Paraphrasing a few lines from that familiar "Children Learn What They Live" by Dorothy Nolte, we can say if young adolescents are taught with ridicule, they learn to be shy, but if they are taught with tolerance, they learn to be patient. If they are taught with criticism, they learn to condemn, but if they are taught with approval, they learn to like themselves. Character is like measles. It can only be caught by close contact with someone who has it.

> *Character is like measles. It can only be caught by close contact with someone who has it.*

So often we, both teachers and the general public, confuse formal schooling with education itself and misunderstand what comprises an education. Education is *not* a process in which somebody does something to or with somebody. It is not just a matter of acquisition. We must never forget that success in adult life will depend more on personal attributes and behavior traits rather than purely intellectual ones.

The real curriculum, the take-home curriculum, includes much, much more than the collective courses of study. Student life, student-faculty relationships, and school policies and procedures all constitute teaching influences. We must recognize the influence of the school as a social system, to what its institutionalism teaches.

Education is really a process of self-development. But what definition of education is learned by pupils as we shuffle them from class to class to learn discrete bits of information?

If your students are the same persons they were when they entered the middle school, except for the addition of information, they have not been properly educated. Students are not enrolled just to learn more, but to *be* more. Ultimately, students assess the options and decide on their own instructional goals. Proper decisions result primarily from their attitudes and aspirations rather than from the correctness of the curriculum as presented by the faculty. Learning is an individual, personal responsibility, and it is value-driven.

Learning is an individual, personal responsibility, and it is value-driven.

In the Sea of Japan there is an unusual species of blowfish. It appears in the waters only once every 11 years, and is considered a great delicacy. While highly sought for its special succulence, it contains a deadly poison. The chef must remove the poison — all of it. If he does it right, it's the best meal you'll every eat, *but* if he prepares it wrong, it's the last meal you'll ever eat.

As educational leaders, are we not all chefs of a sort with the ingredients of an abundant and satisfying school life available to us, ranging from teaching faculties to support staff to a host of technological advancements, such as computers, to the results of research? Our schools, for the most part, are well-equipped and comfortable. Never have we had so much affluence, so many options, so many opportunities, goods, and services at our disposal.

But these same ingredients and opportunities may be underused or misused and become instruments and occasions for belittling students, labeling them, teaching them things contrary to our stated objectives — in short, poisoning students. The difference lies in the attitudes and motives of each one of us, the kind of chefs we are.

The morality of men, women, and children is the key ingredient in a productive and satisfying life. And the values of our schools are showing. Be sure they represent the beliefs we intend to teach — integrity, honesty, tolerance, compassion, respect for the rights of others, civility, self-control, open-mindedness, the common good.

We need to apply our best educational efforts to developing values, that America might progress in morals as well as money, that our students might not only be grammatically correct, but that they would also be good.

The middle school is the best place, perhaps the only place, in which the renewal we need as a people can begin and take root in the coming generations.

The middle school is the best place, perhaps the *only* place in which the renewal we need as a people can begin and take root in the coming generations. If youth are to be more articulate, more knowledgeable, more responsible, if their values are to be more humane, it is at the middle level, not at the high school level, that such goals must be addressed.

As principals and teachers of these key grades you are part of the most important group in our land. The opportunity is ours, the task is clear. Let us begin anew with increased understanding about what we really teach.

Once around the elephant

The Blind Men and the Elephant

It was six men of Indostan
  To learning much inclined,
Who went to see the Elephant
  (Though all of them were blind),
That each by observation
  Might satisfy his mind.
The *First* approached the Elephant,
  And happening to fall
Against his broad and sturdy side,
  At once began to bawl:
"God bless me! but the Elephant
  Is very like a wall!"
The *Second*, feeling of the tusk,
  Cried, "Ho! what have we here
So very round and smooth and sharp?
  To me 'tis mighty clear
This wonder of an Elephant
  Is very like a spear!"
The *Third* approached the animal,
  And happening to take
The squirming trunk within his hands,
  Thus boldly up and spake:
"I see," quoth he, "the Elephant
  Is very like a snake!"

The *Fourth* reached out an eager hand,
  And felt about the knee.
"What most this wondrous beast is like
  Is mighty plain," quoth he;
"Tis clear enough the Elephant
  Is very like a tree!"
The *Fifth* who chanced to touch the ear,
  Said: "E'en the blindest man
Can tell what this resembles most;
  Deny the fact who can,
This marvel of an Elephant
  Is very like a fan!"
The *Sixth* no sooner had begun
  About the beast to grope,
Than, seizing on the swinging tail
  That fell within his scope,
"I see," quoth he, "the Elephant
  Is very like a rope!"
And so these men of Indostan
  Disputed loud and long,
Each in his own opinion
  Exceeding stiff and strong,
Though each was partly in the right,
  And all were in the wrong!

This familiar fable, written by John Godfrey Saxe in the last century, may provide something of a parallel with today's middle level school and its various constituents. With the help of a little imagination on your part, let me explain how the elephant and the six blind men can be likened to today's middle school situation.

While not actually blind, most people who approach the school have inadequate views of this intermediate educational institution.

This article is a slightly edited version of a speech presented at a National Association of Secondary School Principals' Conference in Williamsburg, Virginia, March 17, 1990 and published as the May 1990 *Schools in the Middle*.

The lack of public understanding concerning middle level education continues as one of the major barriers to full implementation of the middle school concept.

But not only is the general public ill-informed, so too is the education profession itself. Indeed, many who are actually involved in it have needlessly narrow concepts of the beast, like the men of Indostan who viewed just one part.

The math department, for instance, may view the middle school as the place where we sort and select students for the high school math sequence. The coach may perceive the athletic program as the farm system for the high school. The reading teacher may see the school primarily as the place where students go to get fixed what's wrong with them.

The academic block teachers may consider the middle school to be the preparatory school for the high school with its expectations of the mastery of various prerequisites. The pressure to cover that textbook content, then, becomes the driving force in their instruction. (Which reminds me of the pointed comment of an eighth grader who was asked, "Are you learning anything in this school?" He replied, "Yes, but I'm learning it so fast I can't remember it.")

Looking at the whole

But a much greater handicap to the development of effective middle level schools is that great mass of us — citizens, parents, and educators alike — who possess ample peripheral vision, yet continue to view it as a collection of separate components.

The middle level school simply is. And what it is, it teaches.

The elephant, you recall, was not properly described by any of the blind men for, when its various parts were viewed in isolation they gave an invalid picture. The elephant is an entity, a big, solid coordinated mass that is seen properly only when viewed as a whole. So, too, is the middle level school. It is not just a variety of classes and activities directed by diverse persons and housed in a common physical facility. The middle level school simply is. And what it is, it teaches.

A school is not significant because it has a guidance program, and an exploratory program, and an academic program; it is significant because of what it is in its totality. Its influence is not determined so much by the length of its course offerings list or the stoutness of its remedial program, but because of its collective behavior, its heart.

> *A school is not significant because it has a guidance program, and an exploratory program, and an academic program; it is significant because of what it is in its totality.*

A school's effectiveness is seriously handicapped when the several parts are not in harmony, and especially when some parts are actually in clear opposition as, for instance, when the affective concerns for developing positive self-esteem are countered by a single, rigidly imposed numerical grading system. But the school, like the elephant, is a single entity in which all systems, all parts, are or should be interconnected, in synch, and which, ultimately can have but one soul.

We must look at the middle level school and its curriculum as a total entity, one that teaches implicitly as well as explicitly. Too long we have addressed school improvement only by dealing with one or more of its parts.

> *Too long we have addressed school improvement only by dealing with one or more of its parts.*

Because we saw, correctly, a lack of concern for the affective domain we inserted a teacher advisory program in which groups met, for example, for 20 minutes three times a week. Because we recognized a need to broaden our recognition program beyond the honor roll we added a student-of-the-week program. Because we sensed some kids were still falling through the cracks we asked each teacher to "adopt" one kid for a semester.

Now we have created another category, "at-risk" kids, and schools are madly scrambling to develop special programs for this newly labelled group. I can't help asking this question as an aside: Have we created another somewhat artificial category, one more basis for further dividing and fragmenting the educational enterprise, another complication for the schedule maker? — and all on the widely held but clearly false assumption that the standard program is okay for most kids? We must face the fact that the only real solution must be in developing a school curriculum that serves well *all* students.

The separate actions we have taken were and are all well-intentioned, and usually to the good, but they perpetuate a piecemeal attack on school reform. Harold Rugg, an eminent professor at Teachers

---

Harold Rugg declared in 1926 that "for over fifty years, tinkering has characterized the attack on the curriculum."

College, Columbia University, declared in 1926 that "for over fifty years, tinkering has characterized the attack on the curriculum." Now 64 more years have passed and literally thousands of projects and millions and millions of dollars have been invested in presumably improving the curriculum — and his assertion is still valid.

Reforming middle level education

Former President Jimmy Carter, when governor of Georgia, tried to institute zero-based budgeting into state government. Although politically, as you might suspect, it could not be implemented, the idea is sound. Typically, next year's budget is built on the existing one. The status quo is the starting point and one adds a little here, quite a bit there, and shaves off just a wee bit someplace else — for psychological effect. But the base is always the current budget and justifications are needed only for major increases. Under zero-based budgeting, however, the starting point is zero. Each dollar, each year, for each item has to be explained and defended on its merits whether asking for more or not.

I have long felt that educational leaders might well adopt the concept of zero-based budgeting and apply it to curriculum development. When considering a change in program, educators always start with the existing curriculum, as if it was semi-sacred and sacrosanct. Then they make adjustments, squeezing a little time from the schedule for a new course, adding another unit to an existing course, but never really tampering with the basic program. Ultimately, about all they end up doing is tinkering.

How true. But the time for seeking educational improvement by adding new courses, new textbooks, or revised courses of study has passed. Tinkering simply will no longer suffice as a means of educational reform. We must, quite literally, first revision, then reconceptualize, and finally restructure.

We must, quite literally, first revision, then reconceptualize, and finally restructure.

To truly reform middle level education we must get down to brass tacks, start from zero, put aside our assumptions about periods, courses, class sizes, even certification fields. The only givens should be our knowledge of the nature and needs of early adolescents, the principles of learning, and the tenets and needs of our democratic society.

If we practiced zero-based curriculum development with those givens, would we ever come up with the program of separate subjects and disjointed entities that we now operate ? Would we ever design that rat race we now provide that has students moving from pillar to post every 45 minutes in an assembly line-like educational model? Surely we would create a better match between the known developmental needs of early adolescents and the educational program provided for them.

If we are to reform our public schools and make them truly responsive to the needs of today's youth and the needs of society we cannot get by simply by doing better what is now common practice. New wine cannot be poured into old wineskins; neither can the needed reforms be contained in the traditionally organized school day.

New wine cannot be poured into old wineskins; neither can the needed reforms be contained in the traditionally organized school day.

Some bold actions are needed. We need to stand back away from school, view it as a whole, be sensitive to the interrelatedness of its elements and remove ourselves from those many momentary problems that hold our attention so that we can contemplate seriously. We must go once, twice, three times around our elephant school with our eyes wide open and think about its place in the total environment, its ecology, its ultimate impact on those who attend it. This is not to deny the significance of its current service or the good that is now being wrought by its caring teachers. We sometimes forget how important schools are in America — even the poorest schools are good for most of the students that attend them.

We all must, however, recognize a major reality that we haven't yet faced. Despite our continued use of the singular, currently there simply is no middle school curriculum, only a collection of separate curricula.

Currently there simply is no middle school curriculum, only a collection of separate curricula.

This is a major concept, and I ask you to consider it thoughtfully. If it is a truth, as I think it is, then we must become, if we are not already, educational philosophers and educational statesmen, as well as educational administrators or instructors. We must grapple with and help others grapple with the tough questions about educational objectives, priorities, and student needs — questions that have no easy answers. We must attack curriculum on a schoolwide basis, reckon with the implicit curriculum as well as the explicit one. We will need to put aside many old assumptions, for as Josh Billings, a character from literature perceptively expressed it, "It weren't my ignorance that done me in, it was the things I knowed that weren't so."

One aspect of restructuring that must be dealt with is the false dichotomy that has been created between academics and exploratories. We continue to refer to them as if they were not only separate programs but were of unequal importance — clearly wrong on both counts. The middle level school is the exploratory school and everything that is done therein should be approached in an exploratory mode.

The middle level school is the exploratory school and everything done therein should be approached in an exploratory mode.

94

At a time when youth's horizons are expanding, their vision broadening, and their curiosity heightened, the school program remains all too narrow, too much of the same in both subjects and methodologies. Middle level education has a horizon-expanding exploratory responsibility that has been underserved.

At best, the basic subjects and the exploratories have remained side by side, not truly integrated. The material studied in the basics is often remote and irrelevant. It usually lacks the emotional tone that the arts, if integrated, could give it.

Schools, society, and values

I can now be classified as a senior citizen. I do not try to hide from that status, but I do try to guard against assuming that posture which is so often associated with the elderly in their views toward youth and the present. But try as I do, I confess I cannot shake the deepening concern I have about the state of our society. And certainly the statistics regarding violence, crime (white collar even more than blue), teenage pregnancy, drug use, child abuse, suicide, etc., etc. lend ample support for my increasingly fatalistic views about where we are headed. A recent survey reported in *Redbook* magazine, for instance, revealed these disturbing statistics:

- Eight of 10 eighth graders have used alcohol — more than half of them by sixth grade. Over one-third had an alcoholic drink last month

- One in 20 eighth graders had used cocaine

- One in 10 preteens has thought of suicide

In light of these and comparable indicators of the state of our society — such as that staggering fact that our prison population has doubled in the last ten years — I believe America is approaching a critical crossroads in what to date has been its phenomenal development as a successful, civilized nation.

Education, inevitably, must play a role in determining which road our nation will choose. In 1932, a leading progressive educator named George Counts, wrote a small book entitled, *Dare the School Build A New Social Order?* Those who answered affirmatively were called "social reconstructionists" and considerable debate ensued as the more traditionally accepted and narrow role of the school as a perpetuator of the status quo was questioned. Call me a social reconstructionist if you will, but I cannot avoid asking a related question in 1990, "Do we dare *not* to seek to build a new social order through the school?" Can America permit its schools to merely mirror the existing society? Shouldn't we vest in our schools the right to try to improve our society?

America desperately needs to renew or reaffirm those values that have been the common denominators of our democratic society.

America desperately needs to renew or reaffirm those values that have been the common denominators of our democratic society. I'm not sure the nation can survive many more decades unless the values that undergirded our society and were largely responsible for its rise to prominence are ingested and then practiced by the younger generations.

In many respects we have become victims of our own success. The material successes gained through capitalism and the high standard of living now so broadly enjoyed have made us self-satisfied. Man's selfishness has been too well served and the common good has been slighted — witness the current state of professional athletics.

The President of Brown University, Vartan Gregorian, claimed that the three scourges in the '90s will be mental gridlock in the form of undigested information, cultural anorexia in the form of self-inflicted ignorance, and national amnesia toward our heritage — a frightening but plausible prediction.

The sociologist Amitai Etzioni claims that America has become hollow, that we have turned our backs on the concept of community in favor of an obsessive self-centeredness and excessive individualism. He says we need to restore "mutuality" and "civility" and reaffirm traditional relationships and shared concerns. Etzioni further says that the school must be rebuilt before society can be revitalized. I agree, except I might reverse or make parallel the two elements and perhaps phrase it thusly: we cannot rebuild schools without also rebuilding society.

But putting aside the chicken-egg dilemma, I am convinced that if our society is to be regenerated, if the old values of our society are to be reaffirmed, the middle level school has to be the birthplace of this renewal. Regrettably, but truthfully, no other institution in our society is in as favorable a position to do what is needed.

> *If our society is to be regenerated, if the old values of our society are to be reaffirmed, the middle level school has to be the birthplace of this renewal.*

We must create in our middle schools an *atmosphere of ethics* where direct attention is given to matters of right and wrong, good and bad, to the ethical aspects of various social issues, where improved *behavior* is the openly acknowledged goal.

While the school's job is certainly not to push a particular religious dogma or narrow set of beliefs it is incumbent upon the school to stand for those many values that *are* held in common by all but the most extreme reactionary or radical. As playwright William Inge stated: "The aim of education is the knowledge not of fact, but of values."

The ancient Greeks advised us "to pay attention to the young, and make them as *good* as possible." Note that they did not say as "smart" as possible or as "knowledgeable" as possible, but rather as *good* as possible. So, restructuring the middle level school means that the development of attitudes, character, and values must be an overt responsibility across the curriculum. Middle level education inescapably is a moral enterprise.

We cannot afford to be timid, fearful of offending in our advocacy of those nearly universally accepted values of civilized living — and I see no real conflict between those values and our strong commitment to being a culturally pluralistic society.

> *There is no conflict between academic effectiveness and developmental responsiveness at the age of early adolescence.*

Nor do I see any conflict between the middle level school's primary responsibility for developing youth's intellect and the responsibility for helping youth develop their values and character. In fact, as I see it, a central tenet of middle level education that needs to be recognized by citizens and educators alike is this: there is no conflict between

97

academic effectiveness and developmental responsiveness at the age of early adolescence. Rather the former can be achieved most effectively only when the latter is attended to overtly. To teach young adolescents the knowledge and skills they need the middle level school must also help them in their social, emotional, moral, and physical development.

Teachers and principals cannot avoid being role models and as such they are torch bearers of a value system, of ethical standards. Unfortunately, there are today, too many torch bearers of other conflicting values prominently on display, which is all the more reason why an educator should avoid being Casper Milquetoast.

The school spirit

The collective attitude of the faculty is the reflection of the values and beliefs of the individual professionals. It determines the culture of the school, its ethos. The students learn readily what their school stands for. The curriculum of climate, I have often said, is as important as the curriculum of content. The school's clout, its power, resides more in its culture than its content. The school itself is a teacher.

The school's clout, its power, resides more in its culture than its content. The school itself is a teacher.

When Lawrence Durrell was writing travel narratives he coined the term "spirit of place" to describe how the quality of place affects us. Place, as Durrell understood, has a major impact on us, and the school is a place, it has a spirit.

Howard Johnston has said, "The creation of the school culture that is necessary to achieve excellence is more dependent upon the behavior of *adults* in the school than on characteristics of students, economic climates of the community in which the school is located, per pupil expenditure, physical facilities, or a host of other demographic-environmental variables."

Think about that — it is a powerful idea. It takes away so many of our rationalizations, nearly all of them, in fact. *The behavior of adults* — you and the faculty — is what matters most. And the key here is not knowledge nor technique, not materials nor courses, but *attitude!* Attitudes more than organizations need to be "restructured."

To change the attitudes of both students and faculty, restructuring will surely have to involve the development of smaller, more intimate learning communities. Such units can enhance student-teacher relationships, aid teachers in knowing students as individuals, encourage the kinds of discussions that will illuminate values and assist youngsters in their social and emotional development as well as in their academic development.

Forming interdisciplinary teams is one major means of moving in that direction, but it is not the destination. The failure to truly integrate the separate subjects when teams are formed is a disappointing reality that disturbs many of us.

Middle level teachers need to be encouraged to step outside of their certification comfort zones and reach for new learnings. Their job will have to be redefined as they move from being presenters of content to becoming directors of learning. They should be able to say to their students, in effect, "You ask of me the way and I point ahead, ahead of myself as well as you. I am a fellow traveler with you, my students, as we pursue knowledge and understanding." Students and teachers need to work in collaboration in deciding on what to learn and how to learn it. We don't just need hands-on experiences in middle level schools, we need hands-joined approaches.

Students and teachers need to work in collaboration in deciding on what to learn and how to learn it. We don't just need hands-on experiences in middle level schools, we need hands-joined approaches.

Increasing the amount of time particular students and their teachers spend together will inevitably move us from the turn teaching that prevails in most teamed situations almost as much as in departmentalized situations. Smaller teams of just two or three and the problem-centered block of time under the direction of one teacher, the real core curriculum, are likely to become more common. So, too, will student-teacher progression plans which keep teams of students and teachers together for more than one year and provide the continuity of caring so lacking in our society.

Conventional wisdom has long taken the position that putting all your eggs in one basket is a very questionable practice. In education, however, I think we've gone much too far in the other direction, in dividing up our educational responsibilities and providing specialized personnel for each facet.

The middle level school should reverse the trend toward specialization and separation. If we put more of our resources in good classroom teachers with reasonable loads and kept them together with a group of students for more than a period a day we wouldn't need so many specialists, each with his or her own little domain and time slot and all adding to the fragmentation of the curriculum.

The middle level school should reverse the trend toward specialization and separation.

Principals have become almost gun-shy because of all the attention given to their importance. In the last decade or so nearly every educational pronouncement has included statements about the key role of the building administrator. They cannot, it seems, escape either the spotlight or the responsibility. But so it is, and so it has to be. Principals are responsible for the physical climate and equally for the psychological climate. They need to be not just administrators but persons who enrich life, create community, establish a sense of mission, instill meaning, and personify the school's philosophy. Faculty morale, ultimately, is dependent upon having faith in the person at the top.

Six blind men, depending on their sense of touch, perceived the elephant in very different, but equally erroneous ways. Parents and educators, though possessing sight, are often partially blinded by personal perceptions and old assumptions, and in their walk around the middle school don't really see it at all.

The time has come to examine the middle school as it is, to view it as an entity, to be sensitive to what it really teaches and what it really doesn't teach, and to understand the importance of having a single, universally understood mission that is evident in every component of the school's program.

*Educators and parents alike must recognize
that the curriculum which counts ultimately
is that one that changes behavior and is still
apparent in the lives of students ten or
twenty years hence.*

Educators and parents alike must recognize that the curriculum which counts ultimately is that one that changes behavior and is still apparent in the lives of students ten or twenty years hence. An excessive concern over the short-term memory aspects of a formal education is likely to be counter-productive. It is all too easy to get up-tight about the fact failures of our youth and institute a narrow plan to correct these knowledge deficiencies. Such approaches are likely to hinder the development of attitudes and values that are of far more ultimate importance.

Certainly, the restructuring road that lies ahead will not be easy to traverse. Although the goal can now begin to be envisioned and there are increasingly more lights along the way to guide our trip, only the most naive would believe the journey can be accomplished without travails and set-backs.

A visitor to the magnificent Cathedral of Notre Dame commented out loud, "Why don't they build structures like this any more?" An old gentleman standing there responded quietly but firmly, "Because those people had convictions. People today only have opinions." That statement carries a message for us. If we are to build the real middle level school, the school that is developmentally responsive and intellectually vigorous, it will take convictions and the courage to carry them out.

Let us then take both as our charge and our personal conviction the words from the German philosopher Goethe: "Whatever you can do, or dream you can, begin it. Boldness has genius, power, and magic in it."

PUBLICATIONS

National Middle School Association
(See 1991 Resource Catalog for member prices)

As I See It John H. Lounsbury (112 pages) $12.00

The Team Process: Third and Expanded Edition
Elliot Y. Merenbloom (173 pages)...................................... $15.00

We Who Laugh, Last Julia Thomason and Walt Grebing.......... $6.00

Life Stories: The Struggle for Freedom and Equality
in America Lynn L. Mortensen, Editor (166 pages) $15.00

Education in the Middle Grades: Overview of
National Practices and Trends
Joyce L. Epstein and Douglas J. Mac Iver (92 pages).............. $12.00

Middle Level Programs and Practices in the K-8
Elementary School: Report of a National Study
C. Kenneth McEwin and William M. Alexander (46 pages)...$8.00

A Middle School Curriculum: From Rhetoric to Reality
James A. Beane (84 pages) $8.00

Visions of Teaching and Learning: Eighty Exemplary
Middle Level Projects John Arnold (160 pages)................... $12.00

The New American Family and the School
J. Howard Johnston (48 pages)..$6.00

Who They Are—How We Teach: Early Adolescents
and Their Teachers
C. Kenneth McEwin and Julia T. Thomason (26 pages)...........$4.00

The Japanese Junior High School: A View From The
Inside Paul S. George (56 pages)..$5.00

Schools in the Middle: Status and Progress
William M. Alexander and C. Kenneth McEwin (112 pages)$10.00

A Journey Through Time: A Chronology of Middle
Level Resources Edward J. Lawton (36 pages)......................$5.00

Dynamite in the Classroom: A How-To Handbook for
Teachers Sandra L. Schurr (272 pages) $15.00

Developing Effective Middle Schools Through Faculty
Participation: Second and Enlarged Edition
Elliot Y. Merenbloom (122 pages)......................................$8.50

Preparing to Teach in Middle Level Schools
William M. Alexander and C. Kenneth McEwin (64 pages)...$7.00

Guidance in the Middle Level Schools: Everyone's
Responsibility Claire Cole (31 pages)................................$5.00

Young Adolescent Development and School Practices:
Promoting Harmony John Van Hoose and
David Strahan (68 pages) $7.00

When the Kids Come First: Enhancing Self-Esteem
James A. Beane and Richard P. Lipka (96 pages) $8.00

Interdisciplinary Teaching: Why and How
Gordon F. Vars (56 pages)..$6.00

Cognitive Matched Instruction in Action
Esther Fusco and Associates (36 pages)................................$5.00

The Middle School Donald H. Eichhorn (128 pages)................$6.00

Long-Term Teacher-Student Relationships: A Middle
School Case Study Paul George (30 pages) $4.00

Positive Discipline: A Pocketful of Ideas
William Purkey and David Strahan (56 pages)....................$8.00

Teachers as Inquirers: Strategies for Learning With and
About Early Adolescents Chris Stevenson (52 pages)............$7.00

Adviser-Advisee Programs: Why, What, and How
   Michael James (75 pages)...$9.00

What Research Says to the Middle Level Practitioner
   J. Howard Johnston and Glenn C. Markle (112 pages)............$8.00

Evidence for the Middle School
   Paul George and Lynn Oldaker (52 pages) $6.00

Involving Parents in Middle Level Education
   John W. Myers (52 pages) $6.00

Perspectives: Middle Level Education
   John H. Lounsbury, Editor (190 pages) $10.00

This We Believe NMSA Committee (24 pages).......................$3.50

Teacher to Teacher Nancy Doda (64 pages) $6.00

Early Adolescence: A Time of Change-Implications
   for Schools Videocassette (37 minutes)..............................$75.00

Early Adolescence: A Time of Change-Implications for Parents
   Videocassette and Utilization Guide (50 minutes).............. $80.00

NMSA, 4807 Evanswood Drive, Columbus, Ohio 43229-6292
(614) 848-8211   FAX (614) 848-4301